PAPUA NEW GUINEA

Language

Grade 8

Teacher Resource Book

Susan Baing

OXFORD

Level 8, 737 Bourke Street, Docklands, Victoria 3008, Australia

Oxford University Press is a department of the University of Oxford. It furthers the University's objective of excellence in research, scholarship, and education by publishing worldwide in

Oxford New York

Auckland Cape Town Dar es Salaam Hong Kong Karachi Kuala Lumpur Madrid Melbourne Mexico City Nairobi New Delhi Shanghai Taipei Toronto

With offices in

Argentina Austria Brazil Chile Czech Republic France Greece Guatemala Hungary Italy Japan Poland Portugal Singapore South Korea Switzerland Thailand Turkey Ukraine Vietnam

OXFORD is a trademark of Oxford University Press in the UK and in certain other countries

First published 2006
Reprinted 2007, 2008 (twice), 2009, 2010, 2013, 2014, 2023 (D)

ISBN 978 0 19 555523 3

Typeset by Polar Design Pty Ltd
Printed and bound in Australia by Ligare Book Printers Pty Ltd

Contents

Chapter 1: Overview **1**

Introduction 1
Key features of the Student Book 1
Key features of the Teacher Resource Book 2
How to use the Teacher Resource Book 2
  Learning outcomes 2
  Outcomes-based education 2
  Learning and teaching strategies 3
  Teaching methods 3
  Planning guidelines 4
  Assessment purpose 4
  Assessment methods 4
  Some useful addresses 5

Chapter 2: Speaking and listening (chapters 1–4) **6**

About this strand 6
Key words 7
Links to other main subjects 7
Possible assessment tasks 8
Teacher information 12

Chapter 3: Reading (chapters 5–8) **24**

About this strand 24
Key words 25
Links to other main subjects 25
Possible assessment tasks 26
Teacher information 30

Chapter 4: Writing (chapters 9–12) **37**

About this strand 37
Key words 38
Links to other main subjects 38
Possible assessment tasks 39
Teacher information 40

Appendices **46**

1. Lesson planning table 46
2. Yearly plan 47
3. Term plan 47
4. Lesson plan 47
5. Assessment strategies 48
6. Answers to activities in the Student Book 50
7. Glossary 63

Overview

Introduction

This Teacher Resource Book is for teachers to use with the *Language for Grade 8, Outcomes Edition* Student Book. It will help teachers implement the *Language Grade 8 Syllabus 2003 for Upper Primary Students* by providing teachers with:

- information for planning a school-based program,
- a selection of teaching and learning strategies,
- a range of planning and assessment techniques, and
- ways to extend and develop content and student practice from the Student Book.

Key features of the Student Book

The Student Book is designed to help students achieve the outcomes given in the syllabus. Students will find models, examples and exercises to help them with the knowledge, skills, processes and attitudes as outlined in the syllabus. Speaking and listening, reading and writing skills are integrated. Students will find meaningful contexts to:

- use language effectively,
- increase their knowledge of language, and
- understand how language works.

The content of the Student Book:

- supports the *Language Grade 8 Syllabus 2003* by following the sequence of strands and sub-strands, while providing integration between strands and sub-strands,
- contains references to the *Upper Primary Language Syllabus* at the beginning of each chapter to show the clear relationship between the Student Book and the syllabus,
- provides four chapters for each of the strands of speaking and listening, reading, and writing,
- covers the sub-strands of production, skills and strategies, context and text, and critical literacy,
- provides topics and learning approaches that directly support the achievement of syllabus outcomes,
- includes a wide range of models, examples, exercises and activities that are student-centred and provide a context for whole language learning,
- is presented in language appropriate for Grade 8 language learning,
- provides models and examples from Papua New Guinea that follow syllabus guidelines (*our way of life: cultural, multicultural, ethical, moral and showing values;* and *integrated human development: the right to healthy living, citizenship, sustainability*),
- uses language that is gender-sensitive and includes positive gender roles,
- uses illustrations to help students understand the text and to stimulate their imaginations, and
- allows students and teachers to supplement materials with other appropriate models and examples in English, Tok Pisin or vernacular languages.

Key features of the Teacher Resource Book

Each chapter contains the following sections:

- about this strand (the role of the strand in a language program),
- key words (major words that students and teachers will be using throughout the chapter),
- links to other main subjects in the curriculum,
- possible assessment tasks (suitable to assess the skills learnt for the strand), and
- teacher information (added information for teachers in terms of specific content).

The Teacher Resource Book is designed to help teachers use the Student Book to successfully implement the *Upper Primary Language Syllabus 2003 for Grade 8*. Key topics are:

- learning and teaching strategies,
- planning suggestions and checklists,
- assessment procedures and checklists,
- assessment activities, and
- suggestions about how to further develop topics and integrate speaking and listening, reading and writing skills.

How to use the Teacher Resource book

Learning outcomes

Outcomes-based education is used to identify and monitor progress in student learning. The emphasis is on what is actually learnt by each student rather than what is taught. An outcomes approach means identifying what students should achieve and focusing on ensuring that they achieve the identified outcome. Teachers focus on planning for student learning. Outcomes are written to measure the success of learning. The syllabus gives a series of outcomes agreed to be essential for all students to achieve.

Outcomes-based education

The language syllabus provides the knowledge, skills, attitudes and values that students should achieve in Grade 8. These are expressed as outcomes and indicators. These outcomes describe what the students should know, understand, value and be able to do. They are student-centred and written in terms that enable them to be demonstrated, assessed and measured.

Each learning outcome is illustrated with a list of examples called indicators. These show the kind of things that students should be able to do, know and understand to achieve an outcome. Indicators can be used by teachers to monitor student progress within a level and to make judgments about the achievement of an outcome. Learning outcomes and indicators will:

- give teachers the flexibility to develop ideas presented in the Student Book to meet the needs of their students,
- help teachers assess and report students' achievements in relation to the learning outcomes,
- allow student achievement of the outcomes to be described in consistent ways,
- help teachers monitor student learning, and
- describe what most students will know and be able to do as a result of effective learning.

Developmental outcomes are also included. They aim to develop learners who are able to:

- reflect on and explore a variety of strategies to learn effectively,
- reflect on and explore a variety of strategies to communicate effectively,
- participate as responsible citizens in the life of local and national communities by developing their language skills, and
- be culturally sensitive across a range of social contexts.

Learning and teaching strategies

The *Language Upper Primary Teachers Guide 2003* states:

Language at upper primary is all about teaching students communication skills. To communicate effectively, students need to have a good understanding of a broad range of skills and processes. Language learning focuses on the development of the four key areas of language essential for effective communication: knowledge, skills, thinking processes, and attitudes. These are explained in the Language Upper Primary Teachers Guide 2003 (table, page 2).

When planning their learning and teaching strategies, teachers need to take into account this extract from the National Curriculum Statement:

By Grade 6, English is the main language of instruction across the curriculum. Vernaculars, however, must continue to be encouraged and developed. Grade 8 students must be given opportunities to continue to express themselves in their vernacular or other national languages as appropriate.

Teaching methods

The *Language Upper Primary Teachers Guide 2003* makes clear the key methods teachers should use: Language is learnt when students are actively involved in genuine activities, in a supportive environment, where the teacher responds to students' needs and interests. Vital to this are the key ideas of interactive learning, whole language, and student-centred learning.

Interactive learning

Students learn language by:

- using it to discuss ideas,
- presenting their own knowledge and expertise on a topic and listening to other students present their knowledge and expertise, and
- working creatively from each other by talking to generate, refine and extend ideas.

Whole language

The whole language approach is used (refer to *Language Upper Primary Teachers Guide 2003*, page 3). The skills and processes needed to help students communicate and respond to a wide range of real and literary experiences are emphasised. Students are encouraged to respond to a wide variety of texts. The Student Book provides a wide range of genres for teachers to use and expand upon. Speaking and listening, reading and writing processes are not practised separately but as part of a whole language experience. For example, students could:

- begin with a brainstorming of a topic to be discussed,
- break into small groups to refine ideas,
- present group ideas to the class,
- write their own response to the class presentations,
- read other students' responses, and
- then discuss those responses.

Language learning takes place through communication and the integration of skills and processes. Where possible, the process should be extended to the community, giving students opportunities to use language skills outside the classroom.

In whole language, emphasis is placed on the processes and skills that go towards creating the finished product. Activities in the Student Book are broken into steps to guide students through processes of language production.

Student-centred learning

A student-centred approach is used. It focuses on learning as being the way that students actively construct meaning, and teaching as the act of guiding and facilitating learning by:

- building on students' prior knowledge,
- using the community and its resources to provide opportunities for students to use their language skills,
- providing opportunities for problem solving, decision making and taking action, and
- providing students with opportunities to reflect upon their own learning, knowledge, values, attitudes and language skills.

The role of teachers in student-centred learning is to provide a supportive environment in which students feel confident to produce language. Teachers can use material in the Student Book to create contexts that have meaning and purpose for the students. The teacher plans and models appropriate language forms in context, and observes and supports students. The teacher will intervene as appropriate to provide assistance and guidance. Much of the skills development takes place in cooperative pair or group situations where students consult each other, share ideas and learn from each other.

The *Language Upper Primary Teachers Guide 2003* provides points about the role of students (page 9). Student Book activities encourage students to develop these roles.

The Guide also provides details of key skills and strategies that can be used for each of the strands (pages 10–11) and both general and specific teaching and learning strategies that are appropriate for student-centred learning (pages 14–31). These can be combined with suggestions for learning given in the Student Book, and in the following chapters of this book.

Planning guidelines

The Student Book and the Teacher Resource Book do not provide planning for term, weekly or daily lessons. You need to:

- plan groups of lessons that use models and activities in the Student Book to enable learners to achieve the outcomes described in the syllabus, and
- fit each set of lessons into a short-term work plan.

Use the table in the appendix as a checklist when planning lessons. Note that the assessing process is part of the planning process.

Assessment purpose

The purpose of assessment is to improve student learning by:

- collecting and analysing information about students' competencies,
- providing guidance, feedback and information about students' achievements and progress to students and parents, and
- helping to make decisions about improving programs and classroom organisation.

The activities in the Student Book are designed to suit these purposes.

Assessment methods

Methods chosen should answer the questions teachers ask:

- What do I want to know?
- How will I find out?

The activities provided in the Student Book help teachers assess students' abilities to demonstrate the learning outcomes. The methods used should:

- enable teachers to closely monitor and understand students' progress,
- help teachers diagnose problem areas in both learning and teaching, and
- give learners helpful feedback after every assessment.

Teachers should refer to *Language Upper Primary Teachers Guide 2003,* pages 32–49, for both general and specific guidelines for assessment. Refer to the Appendices for some useful templates.

Some useful addresses

In Grade 8, students will be stretching their research skills and reading more complex texts. Some organisations in PNG can provide material which you can use or adapt as appropriate.

Agriculture and Development

The Publications Section, National Agricultural Research Institute, PO Box 4415, Lae

Greenpeace (Environment and conservation)

Greenpeace, PO Box 49, University PO, NCD

Komuniti Bus Nuis

Published in English and Tok Pisin

Published by Environmental Law Centre in conjunction with Forestry Information Service

Environmental Law Centre, PO Box 49, University, NCD

National Disaster Centre

PO Box 4970, Boroko

Health Department (local)

You could also contact your local Health Department.

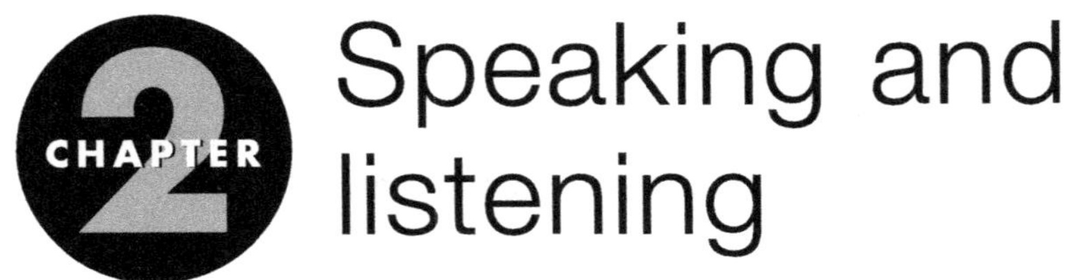

Chapter 2 Speaking and listening

About this strand

Speaking and listening are together as a strand because it is usual for them to happen together. In the four chapters of this strand students will practise activities that lead to these skills:

- listening attentively to follow classroom instructions,
- listening to the teacher modelling speech,
- speaking and listening in discussions,
- speaking and listening in 'read aloud' and 'think aloud' sessions, and
- using language in different ways for different purposes, such as to persuade.

Many of the speaking and listening activities are integrated with reading and writing in both language and other subjects.

Knowledge of texts both written and oral is developed. Students learn how texts are structured in *narrative, recount, report, procedure, explanation* and *exposition.* Knowledge of the written text types is used to prepare for speaking various text types and listening to various text types.

Skills that are relevant to reading and writing underpin oral skills. Students further develop the skills of *generic structure, cohesion, vocabulary, grammar, paragraphing and punctuation, word structure* and *procedural skills.* These are used in the specific speaking and listening skills of *interactive speaking* and *listening, oral presentation, grasping main points of talk, identifying particular details in talk, evaluating and reacting sensitively to what is being said, using figurative language* and *using and recognising non-verbal communication (gestures, facial expressions, body movements).*

Thinking processes that students will be involved in are relevant to each of the strands. They are *decision making, problem solving* and *strategic planning.*

Attitudes are also developed and the syllabus aims to develop students' enjoyment, confidence and independence as language users and learners. They will learn to *appreciate language, interact with others willingly with language* and *show that they have empathy and sensitivity towards others.*

Each chapter covers one of the outcomes. The outcomes can be used to measure students' achievements in creating and interpreting meaning from spoken language, developing spoken language and using spoken language correctly. The indicators are samples of the kind of activity you can use to check if outcomes have been reached. The indicators given in the syllabus have been used as a basis for activities in the Student Book. You should also plan other activities to use as indicators of the students' achievement of the outcome.

The activities and materials in the Student Book are not divided into lessons. A teacher will decide on the outcome to be achieved and then select material to achieve that outcome. Some material may be from different language strands. The templates in the Appendices will help teachers use the Student Book and this book.

Use resources in the PNG School Journals wherever possible to construct similar activities or other activities that help students achieve the learning outcomes.

Key words

These are words or phrases that you as a teacher, and your students, will be using in the four chapters of the Speaking and Listening strand. You will find an explanation of the words in Appendix 7, the Glossary.

Student Book Chapter 1
gentle irony, subtle humour, pun, spontaneous, improvise, message, creative, sensitive, cultural reference, extended metaphor

Student Book Chapter 2
discuss, agreement, disagreement, effective argument, problem, clarify, respect, perceptions, empathy, conflict, reduce, acknowledge, win–win, negotiate, confronting, connotation, so-called, opponent, conciliation, compromise, synthesis

Student Book Chapter 3
manipulate, effect/affect, effective, impartial, impartiality, objective, subjective, challenging, language context

Student Book Chapter 4
satire, powerful, form and function, tense, manner

Links to other main subjects

Throughout the twelve chapters of the Student Book, the first Learning Outcome (8.1.1) *communicate in creative ways, a range of complex issues of local, national and international importance to a variety of audiences* can be applied in most situations. Oral and written communication should follow this outcome. The emphasis on close links with the community is found in the outcome phrase: 'To a variety of audiences'. In Grade 8 students maintain these close links with the community of which the school is part and look beyond the community and nation to the world.

Student Book Chapter 1
Language and culture: Social Science
Cultural change, Activity 8: Social Science
Sympathy and empathy, Activity 10: Personal Development
Health issue, Activity 13: Science, Personal Development

Student Book Chapter 2
Conflict resolution: Personal Development, Social Science

Student Book Chapter 3
Health services, Activity 1: Personal Development
Wheelchairs, Activity 1: Personal Development
Poor baby feeding practice a concern, Activity 3: Personal Development
Land registration, Sir Brian Bell's questions, Activity 5: Current Affairs, Social Science

Student Book Chapter 4
Personal responsibility, Activity 6: Personal Development
How about a cuppa? Activity 11: Making a Living

Possible assessment tasks

Teachers should follow the assessment guides and use the templates in the *Language Upper Primary Teachers Guide 2003*, pages 32–49. On page 49, the Guide states 'Language assessment in the classroom is not about comparing one student to another. It is about assessing the skills and knowledge students have mastered and those aspects they are having difficulties with so that more focussed guidance and attention can be given to individual students.'

Some of the following activities are designed for students to measure their own achievements in terms of the outcomes for Speaking and Listening. Outcomes for Reading and Writing are also included. Students should be given chances to identify their strengths and weaknesses. The tables below will give students an opportunity to do this. Following their responses they can adjust their learning. Teachers can also use the tables as assessment guides.

Assessment for Speaking and Listening activities will take place mainly through observation. You should observe and/or assess students' ability to:

- select and talk persuasively about a range of topics,
- give or carry out instructions,
- talk with effect,
- respond to questions,
- summarise in their own understanding presented information, and
- improvise to express and interpret information modelled.

Language Upper Primary Teachers Guide 2003, page 19.

Activities throughout the Student Book can be used for assessment. Students can also self-assess and be assessed by their peers.

Reading logs and reading journals should be kept. Any writing done should be placed in the students' writing portfolios.

Tests for Student Book Chapter 1

In Chapter 1, students learn to speak with confidence in a number of situations.

As the teacher, you should assess their performance throughout the activities in the chapter. As it will not be possible in terms of time to hear every student present every oral task, you should pick one task that will be formally assessed. Students will also peer-assess. A form to use can be found in *Language Upper Primary Teachers Guide*, page 37.

Listening skills can be assessed by asking the students to write responses to passages you read aloud or record from the radio.

Students can also be asked to write short summaries after they have listened to the oral presentations of their peers.

You can assess the students' active listening skills by listening to their responses in improvisation and spontaneous discussion.

At the end of Student Book Chapter 1, students should fill in this table. Students should tick items when they feel they have achieved the learning outcome.

I understand subtle humour when I hear it.	
I can use subtle humour in different situations.	
I understand irony when I hear it.	
I can use irony in different situations.	
I can listen to a partner in a role and improvise a response in a role.	
I can actively listen and speak spontaneously in a discussion.	
I can speak using imaginative language to create a mood.	
I can identify my audience and speak in a way that they will understand and be interested in.	
I have gained some confidence in speaking to an audience outside the classroom.	

Tests for Student Book Chapter 2

In Chapter 2, students learn about dealing with situations which may become difficult during discussion and public speaking.

Overall indicator: *respond sensitively in a range of different contexts to the demands of audience and purposes.*

Overall indicator: *identify own strengths and weaknesses in composing and presenting oral texts.*

Overall indicator: *develop and use ways of enhancing strengths and addressing weaknesses.*

The above three indicators are not dealt with directly in the Student Book. These indicators should be assessed throughout Chapter 2 on every occasion when the students are composing and presenting oral texts. The indicators are in the table below for students to fill in.

1. Adapting language

Indicator: *adapt language and tone to reduce conflict and acknowledge different points of view.*

Students read the extract *Good cause, but a waste of money* that is found in the back of the Student Book.

1. Students pick out five words or phrases that could cause conflict or are challenging.
2. Students adapt the language and rewrite the text to reduce conflict and acknowledge different points of view.
3. Students should then read their text aloud.

2. Restatement and summarising

Indicator: *restate and summarise main issues to focus understanding.*

Students read the extract *Credit where due* that is found in the back of the Student Book.

1. Imagine you are listening to the text.
2. How could you restate the issue to show that you understand the writer's point of view?
3. What vocabulary and tone would you use?
4. Summarise the main points in the text to show that you understand the issue.
5. Prepare a reply.

At the end of Student Book Chapter 2, students should fill in this table. Students should tick items when they feel they have achieved the indicators of the learning outcome.

I can adapt my tone to reduce conflict.	
I can adapt my language to reduce conflict.	
I can use oral and body language that shows that I understand that there are different points of view on an issue.	
I know how to reach agreement in a group.	
I know what to do if there are disagreements in a group.	
If I am interrupted unexpectedly while I am speaking, I can deal with the situation.	
If I am asked an unexpected question while I am speaking, I know how to deal with it.	
I can see where I am strong and where I am weak in presenting oral texts.	
I am developing ways to improve more on my good points.	
I am developing ways to deal with my weak points.	

Tests for Student Book Chapter 3

In Student Book Chapter 3, students practise speaking and listening to challenging language.

Indicator: *compare and contrast the vocabulary style of spoken language used.*

Indicator: *record own reaction to challenging spoken language.*

Indicator: *detect biased language and stereotypes.*

Indicator: *explain the features of language chosen for effect.*

Read these two texts to students. You will need to read them at least twice. Before reading, tell the students what they are required to do:

1. Ask students to record their reaction to each text in two to three sentences.
2. Then refer students to the texts at the back of the Student Book to answer these questions:

a) Write a sentence or two about the different language (vocabulary and tone) used in each text. (Answer: *Text 1* is more aggressive than *Text 2* and does not give any reasons to support its arguments.)

b) Find some examples of bias and stereotypes. (Answer: for example, *Text 1* implies that all MPs misuse the funds.)

c) Write some sentences on how the choice of words and tone has an effect on the listener or reader, using examples from the texts.

Text 1

A Bill to be presented in Parliament by Andrew Kumbakor hopes to increase the amount of the infamous slush funds available to members for their electorates.

It seems that no Government of PNG is strong enough to take the brave step of ridding PNG of the negative fund. For negative it is, even if it is meant to do good things, because of the way the fund is used.

We know that such funds are now closely watched and accounted for. But no matter how good the system of control may be, the funds are still open to misuse.

To increase the amount for each MP to K1 million would mean a lot more money used in the budget. Is PNG now so rich it can afford this? We don't think so. If this bill goes through Parliament and becomes law, it will spoil even more the reputation of our leaders and our nation.

(part of an editorial, *The National*, 21/09/05, adapted)

Text 2

I support the proposed bill by Andrew Kumbakor. The K500 000 funds given to MPs each year is not enough to deliver services to their electorates.

The electorates are different and the money can do different things in each one. For example, a member in an electorate with good road access to a town can build four classrooms with K500 000, but an isolated electorate with no road access can only build two. The MPs in remote areas get the same as the MPs in Port Moresby. This is unfair.

The critics of Kumbakor should ask him to explain the reasons behind his proposal. Do not jump on the bandwagon just because the media and NGOs are doing it. Kumbakor, you have my support.

(part of a letter to the editor, *The National*, 04/10/05, adapted)

Indicator: recognise the level of impartiality in a news item.

Students read a news item at the back of the Student Book.

They should write a response to show that they understand the concept of 'impartiality', and give examples from the text of its presence or absence.

At the end of Student Book Chapter 3, students should fill in this table. Students should tick items when they feel they have achieved the indicators of the learning outcome.

I am able to identify different kinds of vocabulary style in spoken language.	
I can compare and contrast the vocabulary styles of spoken language and comment on them.	
I am aware when the language I am hearing is challenging.	
I can record my own reaction to challenging language when I hear it.	
I am developing my skills at recognising bias and stereotypes.	
I can recognise language which is being used for effect.	
I can explain the features of language used for effect.	
I can identify powerful language in the speech of characters in plays.	
I can identify how powerful language helps our knowledge of the kinds of characters there are in a play.	
When I read a news item, I can recognise fact and opinion and am able to judge the level of impartiality.	
When I hear different kinds of language, I can explain the language choice and how that language is suited to the context (personal, historical, political, social or cultural).	

Tests for Student Book Chapter 4

In Chapter 4, students observe and use techniques that are used to meet the purpose and shape the understanding of an audience.

Indicator: identify the use of powerful verbs.

Golden Arms by Theresa George

The birds get the sun up	get up—weak > for example: wake the sun
It stretches its glorious hands	stretches—powerful
They begin to part the clouds	to part—powerful
And make them shake their saliva.	shake—powerful
In the valley below it is dark;	is dark—weak >for example: darkness reigns
The village is quiet.	is quiet—weak >for example: slumbers, anticipates
But suddenly the arm shoots in	shoots —powerful
It brightens up with a smile –	brightens—powerful
The dew pools get dry	get dry—weak > for example: vanish
The doors open	open—weak > for example: gape
The chickens go out.	go out—weak > for example: pour out, escape
Your glorious arms bring the golden day.	bring—weak > for example: signal, herald, announce.

The Pacific Series, *Using English, Grade 6, Book 1* (adapted)

1. Students read the poem at the back of the Student Book.
2. Identify all the verbs.
3. Comment on which verbs are powerful.
4. Change some verbs to improve the use of verbs in the poem.

See sample answer above.

Indicator: *identify the use of past and present verbs in different kinds of texts.*

Indicator: *develop awareness of how tense relates to purpose.*

1. Ask your students to find passages from available reading texts (literary and factual).
2. The students copy their chosen passage, then read it aloud and comment on the use of verbs.

Indicator: *demonstrate in own writing understanding of tense in relation to verbs.*

Indicator: *practise the appropriate use of commas.*

1. Set a writing task, such as a report with direct speech.
2. Students should use both past and present tense verbs.
3. Students should use commas correctly.

Indicator: *note where adverbs occur in sentences and how they affect the meaning of verbs.*

Put the sentences below on the board.

Ask students to copy them and make comments next to each sentence on:

a) how the adverbs affect the meaning of the verbs they refer to

b) the position of the adverbs

c) whether any of the verb/adverb phrases could be replaced with a powerful verb/adverb; they should note this and suggest a replacement.

1. The boy ate his food very quickly. a) tells how the boy ate; b)after the verb and the complement; c) ate very quickly (*gulped, gobbled*).
2. You will get a prize if you study hard. a) tells how the study should be done; b) directly after the verb; c) study hard (*diligently consistently*).
3. I haven't done any revision lately. a) tells about time; b) after verb and complement.
4. The river fell quickly over the cliff. a) tells how the water fell; b) directly after verb; c) fell quickly (*tumbled, rushed, roared*).
5. The woman talked softly to her neighbour. a) tells how she talked; b) directly after verb; c) talked softly (*whispered, muttered*).
6. Laka clearly remembered returning the book. a) tells how she remembered; b) in front of the verb.

Teacher information

In this section you will find information on the activities and background to some activities in the four chapters of the Speaking and Listening strand. The information is for you to use, if you wish, in helping you plan your lessons. Indicators are given for some activities. However, these indicators are also covered by other activities in other chapters. Provide extra text material for students to work with wherever possible. New vocabulary should be dealt with in context.

You will find the answers to some Student Book activities in Appendix 6.

Student Book Chapter 1

8.1.1 Communicate in creative ways, a range of complex issues of local, national and international importance to a variety of audiences.

Sub-strand: Production—to provide opportunities for students to use language for real purposes.

Indicator: play with language to display gentle irony and subtle humour.

Indicator: participate thoughtfully and argue opinion reasonably during a whole class spontaneous discussion.

Vocabulary—plan activities if you think your students will need help with any vocabulary in this chapter.

Activity 2: Answer these questions about the jokes and discuss your answers in a group

- Students should realise that it is the unexpected that gives these jokes their subtle humour. For example, when they hear the words *What time is it?* The students would at first predict an answer of time, like *one o'clock*.

For you to try

- Students should try to relate the language plays of jokes and puns to their own Tok Ples or Tok Pisin. Have a class discussion about vernacular humour. Some of the humour could be illustrated as a class display.

Comic strip: this is a pun. Ask the students to discuss the comic strip first.

Draw their attention to the last picture.

The soldiers are asked to come to attention, meaning to stand up straight and salute. Beetle plops down and the sergeant says he has a short attention span, meaning he only stood to attention for a short time. The pun is that *attention span* has another meaning—a person with a short attention span cannot stay focused on anything, such as doing maths problems, for any length of time. Their attention wanders off to something else.

Activity 5: Being ironical

Irony is a gap between what is said and what in fact is true. This has to be fact, not a lie, and it only works if your listener recognises that it *is* irony. Irony is used to amuse or to criticise in a good-humoured way. (Contrast with sarcasm, which is not good-humoured.) For example, if you choke, and someone thumps your back so hard that you fall down, it would be ironic to say 'Thanks for your gentle help'.

Irony is also used to point out that things are not the way they are hoped or expected to be. For example, if it rains on the day of the sports carnival, it would be ironic to say 'What beautiful weather for the sports', when, of course, you wanted the weather to be fine, not raining.

Comment on *Grass-roots cartoon*: the irony is that people complain about Australia but follow the Australian Friday night football like a religion.

Refer to *English for Melanesia, Book 2*, Chapter 18, 'Communicating with Humour'.

Indicator: use metaphor and cultural references to enhance language.

Indicator: create and sustain a mood through the imaginative use of vocabulary.

Metaphor

We often use metaphors when we speak. For example, if we were telling someone that we saw a lot of people watching a fight, we might say 'The people were as thick as ants swarming around the body of a dead fish.' Fresh and new metaphors, such as this example, give colour and life to what we say or write. Metaphors help your audience to enjoy what they are hearing or reading. Metaphors can be used in persuasion. They give us concrete examples of ideas.

Stress the reason for using metaphor—it must be to help the understanding and to increase the interest of the listener or reader.

Activities 6 and 7: Using extended metaphor

➢ The passage is an example of an extended metaphor, where the same comparison is carried on for a few sentences or paragraphs.

For you to try

➢ It will be necessary for you to help your students find possible subjects to be compared. Work with the class and come up with a list from which individuals can choose.

➢ Students should also discuss how metaphor is used in their Tok Ples.

Cultural references—these are clear in many kinds of writing. The original of the passage in the Student Book was referring to the fever that comes on when a black person in America first experiences racial discrimination. This is culturally specific to that context. The story *Conch Shell Never Blows* is also an extended metaphor and the language of the story is enhanced by cultural references and use of imaginative words.

Activity 8: Read a short story

1. The students should first read silently, then aloud in paragraphs around a group.
2. Discussion of metaphor, imaginative language and cultural references should follow.
3. Students should be able to see that the conch shell is a metaphor for the traditions lost during colonial times.

Activity 9: Answer these questions about the story

➢ These questions should be discussed in groups.

For you to try

1. Encourage students to write and speak using references to their own culture.
2. It will be necessary for you to help your students find possible subjects to be used.
3. Work with the class and come up with a list from which groups can choose.

Activity 10: Read this story from the newspaper and Activity 11: Group discussion

➢ Although this is a newspaper story it contains ideas relevant to the indicators. Students should be encouraged to explore their own points of view and feelings.

For you to try

Indicator: raise interest and feeling while in an improvised role.

➢ You may need to lead a class brainstorming session to focus the topic.

Activity 12: Making a table of characters

➢ You may need to guide the students to identify the characters (at least seven) in the passages, for example:

- Passage—former aid worker, starving woman
- Short story—boy, grandfather, modern man
- News story—sympathetic bystander, wantok, human rights activist.

  Students may come up with other suggestions. Sample of information that should be on the table:

- Row 7: character: Gaven, character: person who has died alone; point of view (of author) that this is against tradition; feelings: student's own (should be sympathetic to Gaven).

Improvising in a dramatic sense means to make up dialogue or action on the spot, without preparation.

In the *For you to try* section that follows, students will work by themselves to develop a character. This will be followed by improvisation as a response to a developed character.

Students need to be given some guidance about improvising. Make sure they read all the instructions before beginning.

1. Allow students plenty of time to develop their chosen character. The character could be someone who is marginal to the story, but is a strong 'type'.
2. Before students present their character, tell them that you will later call on someone in the class to respond to their character. This person will have no warning—they will have to improvise. This means they will prepare a character *and* be ready to respond to another student's character.
3. **Give this rule about improvising**: improvisation only works by *accepting and building on* what your fellow performer is saying or doing—it does not work with conflict.

Give this example: act it out with two other students.

Student: I see there are a lot of mangos on your tree this year.
You: No, there aren't. (*conflict*)
Student: Oh, I thought there were.
You: No.
Student: Oh. … well …(dead end)

Student: I see there are a lot of mangos on your tree this year.
You: Yes, yes, there are. (*acceptance*)
Student: What are you going to do with them?
You: Pick them when they are nearly ripe.
Student: What will you do with them then?
You: Well, I'll sell some at the market and the rest we will eat ourselves. I might even give some to you!
Student: I'd like that. … etc.

Activity 13: Getting ready to write a play on a health issue: the dangers of smoking

Indicator: research, plan and deliver creatively and sensitively a message in play form on the danger of smoking to an adult audience.

The key words to be developed are: *research*, *plan*, *creative*, *sensitive*, *message*.

The example of smoking is given in the indicator. If you feel another topic would be more relevant to your students, substitute that topic. The health issue should be one about which students have some access to information.

Students learnt about play-writing in Grade 7. They will need to revise this.

Indicator: participate thoughtfully and argue opinions reasonably during a whole-class spontaneous discussion.

1. Your students have discussed a number of important issues. Plan to have a whole-class discussion.
2. Do not warn the students (the discussion should be 'spontaneous').
3. Begin with a topic and change to another topic when nothing new is being added in the discussion.

4. All students will participate. This discussion should help them to focus and strengthen their ideas on the topics you have discussed in Chapter 1.

Indicator: *compose and present speeches for real purposes at school and in the community.*

Following brainstorming and discussion, students should choose a topic to compose a speech on. The speech should be practised until acceptable and then presented in a real situation as far as possible—the situation will depend on the topic of the speech.

The speech should:

- show a point of view,
- show an understanding of the issue,
- show development of the point of view,
- have concrete examples,
- use imaginative language and metaphors, and
- use humour and irony and show feelings as appropriate.

Student Book Chapter 2

8.1.2 Independently use a broad range of skills and strategies to communicate effectively to groups of varying sizes.

Sub-strand: Skills and strategies—acknowledging the importance of skills and strategies necessary to effectively communicate.

In Chapter 2 students will mainly work towards managing situations in which there is conflict.

Overall indicator: *respond sensitively in a range of different contexts to the demands of audiences and purposes.*

Overall indicator: *identify own strengths and weaknesses in composing and presenting oral texts.*

Overall indicator: *develop and use ways of enhancing strengths and addressing weaknesses.*

Students should be asked to be aware of these three indicators when they perform any oral task.

Indicator: *adapt language and tone to reduce conflict and acknowledge different points of view.*

Students will come up against points of view that are different from their own. These differences can lead to conflict if the students are not aware of techniques and language to use in such situations. Some suggestions are given, but the students need to develop their own means of resolving conflict that they feel comfortable with.

Activity 1: Read this role play in pairs, then discuss the questions

1. Disagreements and arguments must have a set of two or more conflicting assertions.
2. *A disagreement* involves the exchange of two or more opposite points of view (antagonistic assertions) without any attempt to give reasons for the assertions, as in Dialogue 1 of the paired sentences.
3. *An argument* attempts to offer reasons, as in Dialogue 2 of the paired sentences. Of course, this is not a good argument, as the reason is not backed up.

Activity 2: Defining a familiar conflict by group discussion

1. The students will be expected to come up with a personal, individual conflict for analysis by the group.
2. If a student produces a *disagreement* rather than an *argument*, they should be expected to adjust their conflict so that it includes reasons, even if they are not very convincing ones (as in the sample dialogue).

Activity 3: What is the argument really about?

➢ In the sample role play, the problem is that different people have different ideas about using time. Students will copy the table and provide examples from their group discussion.

1. The checklist attempts to find out the different perceptions of the problem behind the argument.
2. What the student sees as the problem in their own argument might be seen differently by other students.

3. When trying to work out what the other person (parent etc.) in each argument thinks, the students will be presuming based on their own life experience.

Activity 4: Reaching agreement by group discussion

- When the problem behind an argument is clear, then you can begin to work towards a solution. The kind of solution you want is one that the people involved agree with. The best solution makes all the people involved feel happy. This is called a *win–win* solution.
- Students will copy the table and provide examples from their group discussion.

For you to try

- Students will apply all the ideas they have learnt so far.
- Check to see that the conflict they have chosen for role play is suitable.

Activity 5: Some ideas for discussion

- This activity shows the importance of communication, especially effective listening, in reducing conflict.
- Students will copy both tables and decide how to fill in columns 2 and 3.

For you to try

Indicator: *negotiate agreement in groups where there are disagreements.*

- Students should use a conflict that is classroom-, school- or community-based, so that they all have experience of the same conflict.

Ways to practise conflict resolution
You can incorporate these techniques when your students are dealing with ways of reducing conflict.
Negotiation
Negotiation is a communication process in which people try to work out their conflicts in a peaceful way using conflict resolution techniques.
Mediation
Sometimes people who want to work out a conflict just can't seem to agree on any way to work it out. They may want another person to help them solve their problem. A mediator is a person who helps two sides to work out their problems peacefully. The mediator helps those in conflict to focus on the problem and not blame the other person, to understand and respect each other's views, to communicate their feelings and what each is really saying, and to cooperate together in solving the problem. Mediators are peacemakers.
Group problem solving
Problems can also be worked out together in a group. Often group problem solvers sit in a circle, so that all members are equals. The same conflict resolution principles are used: they focus on the problem, not on assigning blame to any person; they take turns sharing their point of view, and listening (without interrupting) to all of the other points of view; and all members must show respect and not criticise other members or their ideas.

Activity 6: Using *I* instead of *you*

- To say *I don't like what you are saying* is less confrontational than saying *Your ideas are silly/wrong.*

Activity 7: Choosing the right word

- The words you choose can show your attitude towards the situation. Some words have similar meanings, but may have positive or negative *connotations.* Connotations are the individual feelings we have about words. If you choose the wrong word your listener might react in an emotional way.

Activity 8: Some words and phrases and actions for useful argument

1. Students should talk about how difficult it is, in the heat of an argument, to use these techniques.
2. After discussion, students should report to the class.

3. Students can use role plays to demonstrate the use of such techniques.

For you to try

➢ Students should have an opportunity to put the ideas about reaching agreement into practice.

1. Choose topics that are relevant to your students, that they have feelings about, and that they already have information on.
2. You can have two pairs or four pairs (4 or 8 students) working on the same topic. This will allow students to compare their methods with other students.
3. Students can practise some peer assessment.

Indicator: handle interruptions and unexpected questions effectively.

Activity 9: What can you say?

➢ If possible, listen to Parliamentary debate, or an interview.

1. The polite way of dealing with an unexpected question that you do not know the answer to is to tell your questioner truthfully that you do not know, but will find out and get back to them.
2. Tell students it is best to be truthful rather than pretend you know the answer.
3. Unexpected interruptions should also be dealt with in a non-confrontational way. You could say *I understand your concern, but I would prefer to deal with that point at another time,* etc.

Activity 10: Dealing with audience interruptions and questions

➢ This is a contrived situation. Students will be prepared to a certain extent by reading both texts, which is not realistic. If you can arrange a speaker who is willing to be challenged, this would provide a more realistic situation.

Text B: The Yumi Lukautim Mosbi Projek is a collaboration between the National Capital District commission and AusAID's Law and Justice Sector Program. It is aimed at crime reduction and prevention in NCD, in line with the National Government's Medium Term Development Strategy addressing law and order issues as a means to economic recovery.

Indicator: restate and summarise main issues to focus understanding.

Activity 11: Take notes on each of the texts above and Activity 12: Helping yourself focus

➢ Restating and summarising can be used in two ways.

1. Help your listener focus by telling them your main points again and summarising your point of view.
2. Make points that you have heard clear in your own mind.

➢ Restatement and summarising work both ways: they help both speaker and listener focus on clearing up points that might lead to misunderstanding and disagreement.

Student Book Chapter 3

8.1.3 Critically analyse how spoken language is used in new and more complicated contexts.

Sub-strand: Context and text refers to the importance of learning and using language in different situations and the fact that how we communicate influences the kind of text we use.

In Chapter 3, students will consider language and language context and the effects these have on listeners.

Indicator: compare and contrast the vocabulary style of spoken language used.

Indicator: explain the features of language chosen for effect.

Activity 1: Listen to these two texts

1. The teacher will read these texts to the students.
2. You will probably have to read the texts at least twice.

Speaking and listening

Text 1 'UNICEF paints grim picture of health services', *The National* 24/08/05

(Because of the topic, the language is quite emotional. The listener is left with the feeling that the speaker wants you to take action.)

More than 300 aid posts have closed and more continue to close as Papua New Guinea nears its 30th Independence anniversary, said UNICEF project officer, Dr Anatoly Abramov.

Dr Abromov said the closure of aid posts indicated that vital health and welfare services, especially to mother and child care in rural areas, were deteriorating. He added that the low budget priorities resulted in children dying from preventable deaths. Up to 20 children under the age of one are dying every day from killers such as malaria, diarrhoea, pneumonia, malnutrition, measles, low birth weight and, more recently, HIV/AIDS, he said.

Dr Abromov, who is UNICEF's project officer for immunisation, said last week that since 2001 to 2004 the national infant mortality rate is showing stagnation in its reduction. He said the rapid decline in infant mortality in the 1970s did not continue at the same pace into the late 1990s. In addition the 15% of people living in urban areas are also suffering. The rural–urban drift is seeing people live in poverty.

'Many living in urban areas are financially and socially disadvantaged and live in squatter settlements with poor hygiene facilities,' Dr Abramov stressed. Despite social and economic developments, PNG was ranked 149th in 2001 in the way the government has responded to health needs of the people.

Possible words students will note (others could be acceptable): grim, closure, vital, mortality, stagnation, suffering, poverty, disadvantaged

Text 2 'Charities work on wheelchairs', *The National* 23/09/05 (adapted)

(The listener is left with a good feeling that something worthwhile is being done.)

Two international charities are working with Papua New Guineans to improve the lives of disabled people.

Robust wheelchairs, especially designed to cope with bush roads and rural communities, will be provided to 350 people early next year. Voluntary Service Overseas, an international development agency that works through volunteers, has linked with a charity group called 'Motivation' to bring wheelchairs designed to move around in difficult terrain.

The three-wheeled chairs, made of strong, low-cost and light materials, are easier and safer to use on muddy and bumpy roads and paths than the traditional style of four-wheeled chairs.

VSO country director Dario Gentili said the wheelchairs will help improve the mobility of disabled people. He said 'Those with problems moving around are often disadvantaged by being unable to leave their homes. They do not have the opportunity of education or employment. The wheelchairs will help them play an active part in the community.'

Possible words students will note (others could be acceptable): improve, disabled, robust, volunteers, charity, easier and safer, mobility, disadvantaged, active

1. Students should discuss why the writer of each text chose these words.
2. Students should discuss how the vocabulary of each text compares and contrasts and think about Reading Strand Outcome 8.2.2 (Analyse how a range of literary and factual texts can inform, affect and manipulate the responses of the reader).

Students could read the poem 'Widening Gap' by John Kadiba in *Poetry Speaks*, page 12, and discuss the effectiveness of the language.

Activity 2: Talking about feelings in newspaper items

- Newspaper items can have a big effect on the society of a country because they are read by many different kinds of people. There are two main kinds of items in newspapers:

1. A report on a happening. The language should be objective (without feelings) and impartial (not showing positive or negative feelings). This could be a report on a local event such as a meeting, a sports report, or international news. The writers of reports should only give facts. Of course there will be opinion in a newspaper report when reporters write about what someone thinks, but the reporters themselves must write in objective language (stating facts, not feelings or opinions).
2. A statement of a point of view. You will find opinions given in the editors' comments, letters to the editor and focus articles. Of course these types of items will also contain fact, but the fact is usually written in a subjective way (showing the feelings of the writer).

The two examples show how the writers of reports can influence the feelings of the reader by the choice of language—in the *Post-Courier* report, you feel positive towards the people at the airport; in the *National* report, you feel negative.

Indicator: *recognise the level of impartiality in a news item.*

Activity 3: Analysing reports

- Stress the need to be an alert reader. Students should have more practice at identifying opinions where they should not be given. This is very important because of the role of newspapers in informing large numbers of people. The general population could be manipulated by opinion expressed as fact.

Activity 4: Ranking the newspaper items by the level of impartiality

- Discuss impartiality and objectiveness to make sure students are clear on their meaning. Use plenty of examples.
- Students should look for language which indicates that the writer is not being objective.

For you to try

1. The writing component of this task is based on Writing Strand Outcome 8.3.4 (Analyse how the language and style used in their own and others' writing encourages and stimulates readers to question, develop ideas and opinions and make decisions).
2. Brainstorm with the class to make sure they have topics to suit the activity. The topics can be things that affect them personally, or broader topics.
3. It is important that students read their edited texts aloud to a group.

Indicator: *record own reaction to challenging spoken language.*

Activity 5: Coping with challenging language

1. Students may need help in reading these texts in a convincingly challenging way. Make it clear that they are playing a role—they have to sound like they believe the ideas in their text, even if they do not agree with them.
2. Emphasise to them that they will need to know how to react when they hear texts which challenge their ideas, beliefs, cultures etc.
3. The challenges may be in the form of over-generalisations (or false generalisations) that do not represent the factual position, or in the choice of words and examples.
4. Go through the list of instructions and check to make sure students are completing all the stages.
5. After the final grouping of four students has agreed on the challenges, collect feedback from the class and discuss differences.

Text 1 is strongly written from the point of view of an NGO 'Conservation Forum'. It states 'The Forum and its members do not support land registration'. The views of the Forum are presented in the article. Students need to know that these views are coming from this source and represent the writer's views, not the views of all Papua New Guineans.

Text 2 is the personal point of view of a long-term businessman in PNG. He states that he is not an expert on government finances or planning but writes from his experience.

Indicator: detect biased language and stereotypes.

Activity 6: Stereotypes, bias and generalisations in the texts

- Revise stereotypes, bias and generalisations.

Activity 7: Changing generalisations

- Generalisations are very useful tools in speaking and writing, but if they are not used properly they will weaken the impact of oral or written text. Ineffective generalisations are those that use stereotypes such as '*All* ...' or '*None* ...' instead of making it clear that they are not talking about all of a group.

Read this example from Text 1: *Today, this country has only one thing to be really happy about. It is that the people of Papua New Guinea continue to have customary land tenure.*

This generalisation sounds good. However, the alert reader or listener hearing the words *only one* will think 'this could be an exaggeration'. Ask students what would be better to say instead, for example: *Today, one of the things this country can be really happy about is that the people of Papua New Guinea continue to have customary land tenure.*

For you to try

- Brainstorm to find a number of topics students can choose from. Challenging or controversial topics are needed. They may need to research these.

Indicator: explain how language can be adapted to suit personal, historical, cultural, social and political contexts.

Activity 8: Match the words and the speaker

- Why do we remember these words?

Activity 9: Different language for different contexts

- Students will need help in understanding these arguments, especially in Text 2. However, they will learn some of these ideas from Social Science. Allow time for vocabulary and discussion of the ideas in the texts.
- Teachers should collect other examples.
- How quickly can your students identify the language context? Why?

Student Book Chapter 4

8.1.4 Evaluate how ideas and information have been structured in a range of complex oral texts to meet the purposes and shape the understanding of the audience.

Sub-strand: Critical literacy acknowledges that language learners and users need to think beyond content and recognise and evaluate the beliefs that influence texts.

Indicator: (from 8.1.3) review the power of language combined with characterisation in a play.

Activity 1: Reading a play

- The complete script of the radio play *Which Way, Big Man?* can be found in *Through Melanesian Eyes, An Anthology of Papua New Guinean Writing*, compiled by Ganga Powell, Macmillan Australia, 1987, pages 170–175 **or** the original script *Which Way, Big Man? A collection of plays* by Nora Vagi Brash, Oxford University Press. The script has been adapted to be more suitable for students.

1. This play is a satire on the lifestyle and behaviour of the elite. Students need to understand that the writer wanted to make fun of these kinds of people, so she has exaggerated some of their characteristics. Students should think about the word playing they tried in Chapter 1 and say the names of the characters of Gou Haia and Sinob.

Speaking and listening

What do they sound like? Without actually describing the characters, the writer shows us what kind of people they are.

2. The language in the play is chosen to show the difference between the three characters. Sinob (Snob) talks with exclamation marks and emphasised words (underlined). She uses words that put down people that are not like her. Gou Haia (Go Higher) uses language that shows his ambition. We also wonder if his sympathy towards the less fortunate is genuine—it sounds more like something he thinks he should say. Peta is a servant who is aware of his employers' characters and shows this in his comments.

Other plays that could be used:
'The Long Trousers' by John Kaiwa et al., *PNGSJ Senior 2*, 1999.
'Bun Kakaruk' also by Nora Vagi Brash—adapted from a story. *PNGSJ Senior 2*, 2003. This journal also contains information for students about turning stories into plays. Students can read this to revise the process they will use in *For you to try*.
Students can read the story that was used for the play in *PNGSJ Senior 1*, 2002.

Indicator: identify the use of powerful verbs.

Activity 3: Finding and understanding powerful verbs

- Powerful verbs are those that give meaning and information to language.
- Teachers should look for other examples in texts available to students or the *PNGSJ*.

Activity 4: Using powerful verbs instead of general verbs

- In this exercise students will practise recognising verbs by their function; distinguishing between verbs which could be described as powerful and those that are weak and general; and choosing powerful verbs to replace general verbs.

Activity 5: Verb search

- Students should use the dictionary and thesaurus resources available to them.

Indicator: identify the use of past and present tenses in different kinds of texts.

Indicator: develop awareness of how tense relates to purpose and structure.

Activity 6: Read this story

- Show and discuss how different verb tenses are used in most texts.
- Also refer to *PNGSJ Senior 1*, 1999. 'Voice by the Sea'—show the repeated action sense of present simple: *You can only see her at night.* 'Traditional Fire-making' shows the present tense used in instructions.

Activity 7: Verb or not?

- In Activity 4 students recognised verbs by their function in sentences. In this exercise, some words that look like verbs have been added to refine students' ability to know verbs by their function in a sentence rather than their form. The verb form is being used as an adjective.
- You can give examples from 'Lefaga': *grey-maned, dazzling, shredded.*

Activity 8: Sorting verbs into their tenses

- Discuss with students what the three tenses are and give examples where necessary. Some of the present continuous tense verbs given in Appendix 6 as answers to this activity may be missed by students.
- You can point out that sometimes the two parts of the form can be separated by other words (*are* securely *tied*) and that sometimes the form is not complete. Example sentences:
- I go, (as *I am*) stabbing it …
- I can feel it (*is*) gathering … and (*is*) trickling …

Activity 9: Tenses at work, Activity 10: Checking form and function and Activity 11: Read this article about a young boy

- Students should be able to find and talk about the verbs in the article. Present simple, present continuous, simple past and past continuous are used. There are also sentences using the future tense form *will be ...ed*.

Activity 12: Tenses in the article

- Discuss present and past tense and the two forms, simple and present continuous. Some questioning to elicit answers using the past and present continuous forms will help the students recognise them in the text. For example, What was he doing in the garden? He *was stealing* peanuts. (past continuous)
- Students can discuss the use of the future tense, but will not put it on the table.

References for tense information and exercises:
Literacy Skills for Papua New Guinea, Improve Your Grammar Skills, Units 6 to 12.
English for Melanesia, Book 1, Units 1, 5, 6, 8, 11 19, 20.
English for Melanesia, Book 2, Units 5, 14, 19, 20.

Indicator: demonstrate in own writing, understanding of tense in relation to verbs.

For you to try

- Students can write a story using the visual prompt or choose something else.
- Stress that the correct use of verb forms is important. Although only present and past forms have been discussed in this chapter, they can use future tense forms as well.

Indicator: note where adverbs occur in sentences and how they affect the meaning of verbs.

Activity 13: Finding adverbs

- The adverbs in this extract are formed by adding *-ly* to an adjective.
- Students can search for more such adverbs in their dictionary. Make it a competition to find the first pair of students who can find five such adverbs.

Activity 14: Adverbs and verbs

- Adverbs can help by giving more information about general or weak verbs. Students should realise the continuing need to improve their style of writing. They can search for more such strong verbs that can be used to replace a weak verb + adverb combination.

For you to try

- Another adverb poem can be found in *English for Melanesia, Book 2*, page 130.

Activity 15: More adverbs and verbs

- All the adverbs in Activity 14 and the poem tell how or the *manner* in which something was done. How or in what manner did Tau smile? He smiled *widely*.
- This activity asks students to discover the different kinds of adverbs and note their function.
- You can find more on adverbs in *Literacy Skills for Papua New Guinea, Improve your Grammar Skills*, Unit 15; *English for Melanesia, Book 1*, Chapter 16.
- You should discuss the position of adverbs with your students.

Indicator: practise the appropriate use of commas and full stops.

Indicator: (from 8.1.3) present a critique of a book recently read.

1. Both indicators can be done at any time.
2. Tell students that while they are listening to an argument, speech or other oral presentation, they should notice how the speaker pauses and maybe takes a breath. These pauses help the listener understand the relationship of ideas within a text. A full stop in a written text will mean a longer pause than a comma.

3. Students can use all they have learnt and present an oral book review to the class.

Activity 16: Read these sentences

- You could try reading out some texts without pauses for full stops and commas to show how punctuation affects understanding. Often it will be impossible to make sense of what is being said.
- Here is a famous one—it was used as the title of a book about punctuation. Write the two sentences on the board to show what a difference the placement of the comma can make:
- *A gun-carrying panda enters a restaurant. After a while, he eats, shoots, and leaves.*
- *A gun-carrying panda enters a restaurant. After a while, he eats shoots and leaves.*
- This is also a pun on the two meanings of *leaves.*
- Try this one: *Kylie and Steve took an apple pie juice ham sandwiches fruit salad and ice-cream on their picnic.*

1. Write the sentence on the board.
2. Read the sentence.
3. Students read the sentence.
4. Discuss where the commas should be.

- Did they take an apple, pie or an apple pie? Did they take ham, sandwiches or ham sandwiches? Did they take fruit, salad or fruit salad?
- And these:
- After he had eaten the dog fell asleep. *After he had eaten, the dog fell asleep.*
- Geno was angry at his sister and his father was too. *Geno was angry at his sister, and his father was too.*
- Discuss the roles of the commas and full stops in each sentence or pair of sentences in Activity 17.

Activity 17: Why is the comma there?

- Discuss the three sample sentences in Activity 16 as below. Students then do the matching table.

1. Encouraged by this, Joe did well and won special recognition and applause from the international coffee tasters. The PNG coffee Growers Federation said Joe has the potential to become a coffee taster. *The comma comes after an introductory phrase.*
2. Eee, the sea will stay calm till late afternoon. By then we should be almost home. *The comma comes after an exclamation.*
3. For me,[1] I have one small,[2] but I believe an important,[3] question: how independent as a country,[4] as communities,[5] and as individuals are we? *In the original text, there was a comma before the 'and'. You might like to discuss with your students whether or not it should be there.* 1. for me, *introductory phrase*; 2. and 3. small, but I believe an important, question *comma around information that needs to be separated from the rest of the sentence, or is unnecessary to the sentence*; 4. between items on list; 5. between items on list (necessary?). Note that the comma before 'and' is used when it is necessary to make the meaning clear: The program included songs by O-Shen, Sparky, and Will and Don.

Reference for punctuation
English for Melanesia, Book 2, Unit 9.

For you to try

- This is a summary exercise, and students should be using all the skills they have learnt about in this chapter.

Speaking and listening

Reading

About this strand

When teaching reading skills, teachers need to keep in mind the language principles stated in the *Language Upper Primary Teachers Guide 2003*.

In the four chapters of this strand, students will practise activities that lead to these understandings:

- that reading is for enjoyment, for locating information and for making meaning,
- that good readers know what processes they use when they are reading,
- that good readers know how to make predictions. They base this on what they know about words, about the correct use of words and correct sentences, how certain kinds of writing are structured, and what they know about the topic before they start reading,
- that good readers know that there are several skills they can use to help them find and remember the meaning of what they are reading, and
- that good readers think about what they have read. They make judgements about what they have read. They base these judgements on their own values and on their own experiences of the world.

(based on *Language Upper Primary Teachers Guide*, page 6)

The areas of knowledge, skills, thinking and attitudes are developed in the Student Book:

1. Students' knowledge of written texts is developed. Students learn through reading how texts are structured in *narrative, recount, report, procedure, explanation, exposition*, and *graphic representation.*
2. Various skills are learnt to develop students' competencies in learning and using language in a broad range of contexts: *generic structure, cohesion, vocabulary, grammar, paragraphing and punctuation, word structure* and *procedural skills.*
3. Thinking processes are those in which students' inner ideas, feelings and images are accessed, rearranged and presented. The processes of *decision making, problem solving* and *strategic planning* are used in reading.

Attitudes are also developed and the syllabus aims to develop students' enjoyment, confidence and independence as language users and learners. They will learn to *appreciate language, interact with others willingly with language* and *show that they have empathy and sensitivity towards others.*

Each chapter covers one of the outcomes. The outcomes can be used to measure students' achievements in creating and interpreting meaning from written language. The indicators are samples of the kind of activity you can plan to allow you to see if the outcome has been reached. The indicators given in the syllabus have been used as a basis for activities in the Student Book. Many of the reading activities in the Student Book are integrated with speaking and listening and writing in both Language and other subjects. You should also plan other activities to use as indicators of the students' achievement of the outcome.

The activities and materials in the Student Book are not divided into lessons. A teacher will decide on the outcome to be achieved and then select material for that outcome. Some material may be from different Language strands. The templates in Appendix 1 will help teachers use the Student Book and this book.

Use resources in the PNG School Journals wherever possible to construct similar activities or other activities that help students achieve the learning outcomes.

Key words

These are words that you as a teacher, and your students, will be using in the four chapters of the Reading strand. You will find an explanation of the words in Appendix 7, the Glossary.

Student Book Chapter 5
respond, response, influence, symbol, theme, sound, alliteration, assonance, rhyme, full rhyme, near rhyme, rhyme pattern, infer, folk saying, proverb, metaphor, alternative, memorable, enduring

Student Book Chapter 6
questionnaire, response, respondent, categorical, scaled, ranking

Student Book Chapter 7
flashback, time period, real time, persona, genres, implications, consequences, green revolution

Student Book Chapter 8
functional language, fluent, source, citing, quote, paraphrase, credible, plagiarism, acknowledge, bibliography, format, futuristic

Links to other main subjects

Student Book Chapter 5

The Outsider, Activity 2: family, self-worth, Personal Development
Island Fire, Activity 3: cultural change, Social Science
Four Orders, Activity 5: usefulness, Personal Development
Dreams, Activity 5: optimism, Personal Development
Folk sayings and proverbs, Activity 11: preserving culture, Social Science
The starfish story, Activity 12: acting locally, personal responsibility, Social Science, Personal Development

Student Book Chapter 6

Indonesian culture, Activity 1: World cultures, Social Science
Chinese culture, Activity 2: World cultures, Social Science
Racial prejudice: Social Science, Personal Development
Stereotypes: Personal development

Student Book Chapter 7

The Fautasi Race: cultural change, Social Science
Huria's Rock: culture, Social Science
King tides, Activity 10: Science
Green Revolution: agriculture, Science
Bird flu, Activity 13: Health

Student Book Chapter 8

Literacy and becoming literate, Activities 1 to 8: Social Science, Personal Development

Possible assessment tasks

The following activities are designed for students to measure their own achievements in terms of the Grade 8 Outcomes for Reading. Outcomes for Speaking and Listening and Writing are also included.

Teachers should follow the assessment guides and use the templates in the *Language Upper Primary Teachers Guide 2003*, pages 32–49.

Some of the following activities are designed for students to measure their own achievements in terms of the outcomes for Reading. Teachers can also use these tables as assessment guides.

Activities throughout the Student Book can be used for assessment.

Assessment for Reading activities will take place mainly through observation of the reading behaviours and strategies used by students at work. Observations take place before, during and after reading. Assessment takes place during:

- silent reading,
- small group interaction,
- shared reading, and
- discussion.

Students can also be assessed through their written responses. Reading logs and reading journals should be kept. Any writing done should be placed in the students' writing portfolios.

Tests for Student Book Chapter 5

In Chapter 5, students learn about reading beyond the words on the page and inferring and responding to different texts.

Indicator: select and read aloud expressively a text which evokes a particular response in the reader, e.g. suspense/tension/sadness, and explain how the author achieves that response.

Indicator: investigate the quality of sound, e.g. assonance, alliteration and rhyme, in a poem and contrast the effects on the reader of its inclusion or absence.

Students will read the poems at the back of the Student Book and answer these questions:

Landscape

1. What form does the poem take? Look at the first line of each verse, then the following lines. *Question and answer*
2. Find one example of alliteration. *footprint, feather; desert sand swirled; mollusc, mammal; sunrise, sleep*
3. Find one example of assonance. *Junk-yard of cars*
4. Find one example of rhyme. *world, swirled; stars, cars; earth, birth; sleep, heap.*

My Land

1. What form does the poem take? Look at the first line, then the following lines. *A sub-title or announcement of the topic*
2. Find one example of alliteration. *silent, sea; creeping, coiling; blooming, bearing*
3. Find one example of assonance. *craters, caves*
4. Is there any rhyme? *not really (coiling, bearing?)*

- Students should write a comparative analysis of the two poems, expressing a preference for one of them.
- They should analyse also what makes them respond in a certain way to the poem of their choice.
- An assessment of expressive reading could also be done.

Indicator: read a news item and in small groups role play logically or imaginatively likely reactions of known or unknown characters.

Teachers could use this activity as outlined in the Teacher Information below as an assessment of the indicator for the outcome.

Indicator: respond to texts beyond the literal level by recognising inference, metaphor and alternative readings.

Reading

Students read the passage at the back of the Student Book and make a list of all the things they can infer from the passage:

1. The woman with the stick is old, is infirm (*walking stick, hauls*), is Tom's mother (*thank you, dear son*), loves her son Tom (*pats arm*), lives with Tom and Maria, is not liked by Maria (*I don't know why …*); Maria is jealous of her (*It's a pity …*).
2. Maria is Tom's wife (*implied*), does the housework (*gathering up …*), she thinks Tom does not show fondness for her (*it's a pity …*)
3. Tom goes out to work (*looks at watch; you'll be late*).

Indicator: reflect, through discussion, on how authors create characters, events and language that lives on after a book or play has been read.

Teachers could use the *For you to try* activity on enduring texts for assessment of this indicator for the outcome.

At the end of Student Book Chapter 5, students should fill in this table. Students should tick items when they feel they have achieved the indicators of the learning outcome.

I can recognise what an author does to make the reader respond.	
I can use this information to read expressively.	
I can recognise the ways a poet uses sound to make the reader respond to his language and images.	
I can express a preference of poems which use or do not use sound devices.	
I can infer information from what is written by using context or general knowledge.	
I can respond to metaphor in a text.	
I understand that texts can be interpreted in different ways.	
I can recognise a text that contains characters, events and language which will have a lasting effect on me and others.	

Tests for Student Book Chapter 6

In Chapter 6 students revise some skills learnt earlier. They also learn more about what makes a good questionnaire.

Indicator: improve skimming and scanning skills for quick and effective retrieval of information.

Scanning

Locate a passage in a text available to all students. The text should contain facts that can be found as answers to questions.

Give students a purpose for reading the article and either prepare questions for students, or get them to write their own questions. You can then also assess the questions they write to find facts for the purpose.

Skimming

Use a text from another chapter in the Student Book, for example, Chapter 3.

Indicator: analyse and discuss reasons for the use of standard, formal and unbiased language in questionnaires and justify, giving examples.

Draw the table on the next page on the blackboard and fill in columns 2 and 3 (answers provided).

Indicator: detect inferred meanings and irony in a selection of cartoon or comic strips.

There are two comics in the back of the Student Book.

Students should look at them and then list all the ironies and inferences.

Bringing up Father

Inference from first speech: the bartender knows the man well, meaning he is often in the bar.

Inference from second speaker: anyone asking for him can't be good—he says 'Uh Oh'.

Inference from second speech bubble of second speaker: he expects that the only reason someone would be looking for him is because he owes money (bill—paper stating amount owed).

Irony: the bartender either mistakes the man's meaning or is deliberately being ironical—in other words, mocking the man because he knows the man owes money everywhere (bill as in duck's bill/mouth).

Question	type of question	problem with question
Do you have a licence?	Categorical	ambiguous, unclear—what kind of licence?
What are the main crimes committed by people who live in squatter settlements?	Open-ended	makes judgements, calls on feelings or is offensive Respondent may not know answer
Should the city get rid of any people who are beggars and nuisances? strongly agree ____, agree ____, no opinion ____, disagree ____, strongly disagree ____	Scaled	uses strong words that might influence the respondent
How often do you like to spin after school? Tick one. every day ____ 2–3 times a week ____ once a week _____ never ______	Checklist questions	using slang language
What is your choice for lunch food in the canteen? Put the choices in order from first choice to last choice. sausages and chips ____ bananas and greens ____ kaukau and pumpkin ____ sandwiches and biscuits ____ chicken and kaukau ____ lamb flap and pumpkin ____	ranking	uses double answers—the respondent may not be able to choose any or rank them effectively
Are you an old person?	fill-in questions	too personal, could be offensive, what is old?

Reading

Redeye

Irony: he may not be able to write but he can make a 'note' (musical).

Inference from first speaker: there will be a 'note'. He expects what he sees in the smoke signal that goes up.

Inference from second speaker: There will be no note because 'Tanglefoot' is illiterate.

Inference from second speaker: you have to be able to spell to send smoke signals.

Irony: smoke signals form messages through the number and size of smoke puffs used, not letters or words or symbols.

At the end of Student Book Chapter 6, students should fill in this table. Students should tick items when they feel they have achieved the indicators of the learning outcome.

I understand that scanning and skimming have different purposes.	
I can use scanning appropriately to find information.	
I can use skimming appropriately to find information.	
I can use the correct questionnaire format.	
I can analyse the language used in questionnaires and use appropriate language.	
I am improving my skills in recognising irony.	
I am improving my skills in making inferences.	
I am improving my skill in interpreting how stereotypes are used in texts.	
I can debate issues raised in a non-biased and objective manner.	
I can use vocabulary from other subjects I study in debate.	

Tests for Student Book Chapter 7

In Chapter 7, students learn more about various genres, especially narratives.

Indicator: gather examples from different authors' work and note how they handle time and demonstrate knowledge of these in creating own narrative.

Teachers can use the students' analysis of time in their written narrative to assess their understanding of the role of time in a narrative.

There are also many stories in the *PNG School Journals* (Senior) that can be used.

Select five stories and ask students to analyse the use of time in those stories following a pattern of questioning similar to that in Chapter 7, Activities 2–8.

Indicator: consolidate, by reading more complex examples, knowledge of different genres including persuasive/discursive/explanatory/instructional texts, and use appropriate features in own writing, justifying own choice of genre.

Provide 10–20 examples from the *PNGSJ* and number them. Students are to write what genre these texts belong to, and indicate what it is about the text that is specific to that genre.

Indicator: read about a decision made on a locally relevant issue and analyse possible implications.

Provide a relevant and appropriate text from the newspaper that gives a decision. Students will think of implications of making or not making that decision.

At the end of Student Book Chapter 7, students should fill in this table. Students should tick items when they feel they have achieved the indicators of the learning outcome.

I am aware of how an author can present time differently and the reasons for this.	
I am aware of flashbacks and their role in narratives.	
I can show my knowledge of how time can be handled in a text when I write my own narratives.	
I know the features of the following genres: persuasive, explanatory, instructional, narrative.	
I can recognise these genres when I read them.	
I can show my knowledge of genres by using the appropriate generic structures when I write.	
I can analyse the implications of a written decision.	

Tests for Student Book Chapter 8

In Chapter 8, students learn to further develop their research skills.

Indicator: write a concise and accurate synthesis of research undertaken from demanding reading material, crediting the views gathered.

Indicator: draft a set of main points, including relevant evidence from reading, to be used in leading and guiding a peer group discussion on an important local social issue.

1. Students can be assessed on the bibliography writing skills.
2. The stages of preparation and discussion that result from research should be assessed progressively.

Indicator from Chapter 7: crucially examine and discuss the language of advertising; read and note down relevant persuasive features and personal responses.

Indicator: select a claim or promise in an advertisement and write a futuristic story about the reader who has bought the advertised product or services.

Provide two advertisements for students to analyse. One should be an informative advertisement, the other a persuasive advertisement.

Indicator: read a news item of a current event and devise a relevant humorous or ironic cartoon or comic strip.

The cartoon or comic should be assessed.

At the end of Student Book Chapter 8, students should fill in this table. Students should tick items when they feel they have achieved the indicators of the learning outcome.

I am aware of the importance of research in preparation for my own writing, speech making or discussion preparation.	
I can correctly record my sources for research in a bibliography.	
I can prepare for a discussion and take part in a discussion using my prepared notes.	
I can identify the features of both informative and persuasive advertising.	
I can use an advertisement to write an imaginative piece.	
I can use a news item to write a cartoon or comic strip.	

Teacher information

In this section you will find information on the activities and background to some activities in the four chapters of the Reading strand. The information is for you to use, if you wish, in helping you plan your lessons.

There are some key skills and processes that teachers need to use for teaching reading using the Student Book. These key skills and processes apply to any reading task you give your students.

Reading effectively means using a three-stage process. Each time a reading task is approached, decide how you can best use these three stages:

1. Before they read students should:
   - look,
   - talk,
   - share their ideas in a pair or group situation, and
   - make predictions about any text and any diagrams, graphs or pictures that accompany the text.
2. During reading students should:
   - join in the reading,
   - read on further in the text or read back in the text,
   - use pictures or graphs that accompany the text to help them interpret the text,
   - make mental pictures of their own,
   - attempt to clarify what they are reading,
   - make use of cues from the meaning of words, the sounds of letters and letter groups and grammatical structures of sentences, and
   - attempt to sound out and discover the meaning of unknown words.
3. After reading students should:
   - talk about what they have read,
   - think about the content, ideas and issues in what they have read,
   - share their thoughts with other students in a pair or group situation,
   - compare their own thoughts with other students and justify their ideas,
   - practice substituting words or ideas or writing new endings to stories,
   - go beyond the text they have read and make comments, and
   - analyse the content.

The *Language Upper Primary Teachers Guide 2003*, pages 19–27, provides reading strategies for the teacher to use in teaching reading. These can be applied to the activities in the Student Book.

You will find the answers to Student Book activities in Appendix 6.

Student Book Chapter 5

8.2.1 Read, reflect and respond critically to a broad range of complex literary and factual texts.

Sub-strand: Production—to provide opportunities for students to use language for real purposes.

Indicator: select and read aloud expressively a text which evokes a particular response in the reader, e.g. suspense/tension/sadness, and explain how the author achieves that response.

Activity 1: Reading and responding to a story, Activity 2: Reading and responding to another story and Activity 3: Reading and responding to a poem

➢ Students should analyse what their response is and try to find what it is in a text that leads them to that response. Note that it is not language alone that determines response—images, symbols and the students' own experiences all play a role.

Reading

- Once they have identified their response they can read the text aloud with the appropriate expression.
- Any of the other texts in this chapter can be used to practise the skills further.
- In *Island Fire*, the poet expresses sadness at the changes in the traditional way of life. She gives three examples of activities people do at night now, which they did not do before: billiards, 'Hollywood' on TV, and modern music. She also depicts children getting a 'foreign' education. The title symbolises traditional culture. Only its 'embers' remain, meaning that it has almost 'gone out'. If culture is only rekindled by 'kerosene' (a symbol of modern ways), this means it will no longer be traditional. The 'dry coconut leaves' (symbolising traditional ways) should be used instead, even though it will take more effort.

Indicator: investigate the quality of sound, e.g. assonance, alliteration and rhyme, in a poem and contrast the effects on the reader of its inclusion or absence.

Activity 4: Responding to alliteration and assonance, Activity 5: Responding to rhyme and Activity 6: Poem summary

- Students have learnt about the skills of identifying poetic devices in previous years. Revise as appropriate.
- Refer to *Poetry Speaks*, Leone Peguero and Ganga Powell, Heinemann Education Australia, 1988; *English for Melanesia Books 1 and 2.*
- All of the poems must be read aloud.

Indicator: respond to texts beyond the literal level by recognising inference, metaphor and alternative readings.

Often readers are given a limited amount of information. The reader then makes inferences from the information given. This is a thinking or reasoning skill. Readers can infer using context clues or general knowledge.

Activity 7: What do you infer?

- Students can be given more such choices to practise the skill. They can also write similar activities to test their partners.

Activity 8: Making inferences in a longer passage

- You can use any passage from a text that the students are currently reading.
- Related skills are using context clues and drawing conclusions.

Activity 9: Read this passage

- The *Rice Without Rain* text will need to be discussed with the class to help with understanding.

Activity 10: Metaphors, Activity 11: Proverbs and Activity 12: Inference and metaphor in a story

- Students have learnt about metaphors in Grade 7. Revise as appropriate.
- Students can put together a booklet of metaphorical folk sayings from their cultures.
- Discuss how stories, poems or plays can be interpreted in different ways by different people. Some people can see the literal meaning of a story, but have problems looking beneath the surface at the figurative meaning. Figurative interpretations can also be different from person to person depending on the life experiences they have had and their general knowledge. This is something students need to keep in mind when thinking about audience as they do the *For you to try* activity.

Indicator: reflect, through discussion, how authors create characters, events and language that live on after a book or play has been read.

Classic literature is often cited as enduring literature. However, any text your students read qualifies if they remember the characters, descriptive passages or language use.

Students should also be able to identify and discuss what it is that makes a text live on in their minds.

Indicator: read a news item and in small groups role play logically or imaginatively likely reactions of known or unknown characters.

No activity is given in the Student Book for this indicator as it will be more effective to use a current issue reported in the newspaper.

The teacher can allow students to choose an issue reported, or all students can be given the same issue or select from a range of issues.

The report does not need to have characters, though dialogue in a report can be used in the play. Students will put forward their own characters, and make their speech and action show the characters' reaction to the news item.

They will use all they have learnt so far about writing and performing role plays.

Student Book Chapter 6

8.2.2 Analyse how a range of literary and factual texts can inform, affect and manipulate the responses of the reader.

Sub-strand: Skills and strategies—acknowledging the importance of skills and strategies necessary to effectively communicate.

Indicator: improve skimming and scanning skills for quick and effective retrieval of information.

This technique can be practised any time you want pupils to find facts quickly, for example in Social Science. The only way to actually improve their reading speed and information location skills is to constantly practice.

Activity 1: Using scanning skills and Activity 2: Skimming skills

- The two articles are included for students to practise the scanning and skimming skills they learnt in Grade 7. You should provide other suitable texts.

Indicator: analyse and discuss reasons for the use of standard, formal and unbiased language in questionnaires and justify, giving examples.

Refer to *English for Melanesia Book 2*, pages 57–68

A questionnaire is used to find out information for a specific purpose. It is a number of questions put together in order to investigate something. This can be to find out the behaviour, opinions, knowledge of facts and so on of a group of people, especially as part of a survey.

A survey is often useful for decision making. A survey can tell you things that you will not find out in any other way. This means the language used in surveys must be carefully chosen.

Students will learn to focus on an issue to be investigated.

Activity 3: Answering a questionnaire

- This is designed to let the students fill in a prepared questionnaire and to be used as a model for their own questionnaires. Discuss each question so they are sure of how to fill in the answers.

Activity 4: Types of questions in a questionnaire

- Students have learnt about closed and open questions in Grade 7.

Closed questions are also called pre-coded or structured. They give the respondent a limited number of choices when answering. This type of question is easy to answer and easy to record. However, sometimes it does not provide enough data.

Open questions are also called open-ended or unstructured. They ask for the respondent's opinion and are more flexible. However, too many open questions can discourage respondents from completing the questionnaire. Also, they take more time to answer and more time to score.

- In filling in the table students should write the question number (1–6) in the appropriate space. Discuss the answers and look at each question in detail.

Activity 5: Things to look out for in how you write questions

➢ Analyse each question to point out what the problem is.

1. Unclear questions: To what extent would you use the library? (What does 'extent' mean in this context?) The question does not define what answer is wanted.
2. Questions that ask the person filling in the questionnaire (*respondent*) to remember things: How many books did you read last year? The respondent will not be able to give an accurate answer.
3. Questions that ask for an answer the person filling in the questionnaire may not know: How many books are there in the school library? The respondent will not be able to give an accurate answer.
4. Double questions: Do you like newspaper and books? The respondents might like one but not the other—how then would they answer?
5. Questions which lead the person filling in the questionnaire towards an answer: Do you think libraries are useful? The respondents might think they had to answer yes.
6. Do not use language that is hard to understand: Do you ever use the Dewey decimal system to locate a book? The respondent will not be able to give an accurate answer.

Activity 6: Discussion questions

➢ Allow time for the discussion questions in groups.

- Why is it necessary to use unbiased language in questionnaires? The respondent should not be influenced by the language of the questionnaire.
- Why is it important that the language of your questions is not ambiguous? An unclear question will lead to an unclear answer.
- Why is it important to avoid leading questions (questions that seem to want the respondent to answer in a certain way)? The idea is to get accurate responses.
- Why is it important to avoid using strong words that might influence the respondent, such as *highly effective government, prompt and reliable*? The idea is to get accurate responses.
- Why should you avoid using language that makes judgements, calls on feelings or is offensive? You could affect the answers.
- Why should you avoid slang and instead use more formal language? A questionnaire is a formal document.
- Why should you avoid using language that is specific to your culture? Your respondent may not understand the cultural reference.
- Why should you avoid using technical language? The respondent may not understand and thus will not answer accurately.

For you to try

➢ You may want your students to put a written questionnaire into practice. Remember in this case the questionnaire is not an instrument to use in an interview—it should be distributed and then collected later.

➢ Students should discuss possible challenges/problems with this way of gathering information, such as:

- many people are not literate,
- some questions in multiple choice might not cover all the possible choices for a respondent,
- questionnaires take a lot of time and resources to get ready,
- they take a lot of time to analyse,
- your respondents can only answer the questions that are on the questionnaire—they can't give extra information, and
- many people don't like answering questionnaires.

Indicator: use subject-specific vocabulary during a whole-class debate.

Indicator: show skill in expressing opinion in a non-biased, objective manner.

- Students learn about systems of government, decolonisation, globalisation, historical societies and many other topics in Grade 8 Social Science that use subject specific vocabulary.
- A debate can be organised in which students are required to use subject-specific vocabulary, or language and expressions that are specific to various topics.
- Information gathered by the students in their questionnaires may lead to debate or speech making.

Indicator: detect inferred meanings and irony in a selection of cartoon or comic strips.

Activity 7: Irony in comics and cartoons and Activity 10: Inference in comics

- Students must go on from answering the questions to a general discussion of irony and inferred meanings. What is the role of irony? Why do we find inferences that go wrong funny?

Activity 8: Inferring from a poem and Activity 9: Poem discussion

- Allow time for answering the questions and discussion. Some students will be able to infer that this is Jesus from the first verse. Others may take longer. There are plenty of clues. Emphasise the need to be an active and thinking reader—what is behind the words?

Indicator: interpret the use of stereotypes in texts showing an understanding of the reasons for their use.

Activity 11: Stereotype labels and Activity 12: Some stereotypes

- Discuss why it is not appropriate to use labels like this.
- Make a class list of PNG stereotypes. Emphasise that this does not mean that all people in PNG are like this.
- What use do stereotypes have? They are good in argument, to make a point strongly, but can be easily disproved.

Indicator: clarify the strength or the weakness of a read argument, forecast an opposing view and express this in a letter.

This indicator is dealt with in Chapter 12, where relevant writing is done.

Student Book Chapter 7

8.2.3 Analyse and justify personal preference for authors, styles, themes and other features in a range of literary and factual texts.

Sub-strand: Context and text refers to the importance of learning and using language in different situations and the fact that how we communicate influences the kind of text we use.

Indicator: gather examples and note how, from different authors' work, they handle time and demonstrate knowledge of this in creating own narrative.

As students read the stories, take the opportunity to remind them that the author is not giving all the information; the reader has to infer some things. Talk about whether or not this makes it more interesting. Use the questions in Activities 2, 4 and 6 to start discussion.

Activity 1: Time in a story 1

- The first story, *The Old Truck*, begins and ends within a few minutes. There are no flashbacks or gaps in the story. The following stories have progressively more complicated time frames.

Activity 3: Time in a story 2

- In *The Handy Man*, there is a gap in time between Craig being told the places he cannot fix the bike and the telephone call from Don after lunch. Apart from that there is a straight chronological timeline.

Activity 5: Read this story

- There is a flashback in *The Fautasi Race*, and the story covers a longer period of time, with gaps where the reader does not know or need to know what is happening in these characters' lives.

Activity 7: Read this story

- *Huria's Rock* covers a short time period, similar to *The Old Truck*. However, it is a longer story, more complicated, and there is a flashback.

Activity 9: Time lines for stories

- Talk in general about the role of time in narratives. You may have watched films together that have flashbacks.
- You can also take time to talk about *persona*, or the person in the story whose point of view is shown. Get students to recognise who is the voice in the four stories—is it the author herself? Or has the author spoken as an adopted persona? Is there any way of telling which is which? What effect does this have on the narrative?

Indicator: consolidate, by reading more complex examples, knowledge of different genres including persuasive/discursive/explanatory/instructional texts and use appropriate features in own writing justifying own choice of genre.

- Revise genre by getting students to prepare lists of all genres they think they know.
- Not all genres can be represented in the Student Book. Make good use of the *PNG School Journal* (Senior).

Indicator: examine and discuss the language of advertising; read and note down relevant persuasive features and personal responses.

- This indicator will be dealt with in Chapter 8.

Indicator: read about a decision made on a locally relevant issue and analyse possible implications.

- Some samples of decisions are given. Students should discuss these samples. Then they should seek out decisions on locally relevant issues: it could be to improve a road, downgrade an airstrip, or raise fees at the market. If you cannot go to decision-making bodies outside the school, you could discuss in-school decisions.

Activity 12: Thinking about what decisions mean

Whenever a decision is made there will be implications or consequences. For example, a student might decide not to study for a test. The result will most likely be a lower mark. You and your students will frequently read about decisions in the newspaper Sometimes the implications are clear, sometimes the reader will have to think of the implications themselves. This is a reading skill that uses reasoning.

- Discuss the difference between the green revolution as defined in the article (Text 3) and the 'green revolution' as it seems to be happening in PNG.
- What are your and the students' feelings about some controversial ideas in this article?
- Note that the implications of a decision also include the implications of not making that decision.

Activity 13: Implications of a health decision and Activity 14: Implications of an economic decision

- Fully discuss all implications for all parties involved.

Student Book Chapter 8

8.2.4 Analyse how an author's choice of language and style encourages and stimulates readers to question, develop ideas and opinions, and make decisions

Sub-strand: Critical literacy—selecting and evaluating information researched, leading to making informed choices and opinions.

Indicator: Write a concise and accurate synthesis of research undertaken from demanding reading material, crediting the views gathered.

Indicator: Draft a set of main points, including relevant evidence from reading, to be used in leading and guiding a peer group discussion on an important local social issue.

Four different kinds of texts are provided. These will help students learn the basic research skills. Take time to make sure students understand the information in each kind of text.

For their own research they should be helped to choose a topic about which they can find some basic information.

Some background on policy is shown in the table below.

Activity 10: Your list of sources

- There is no one definite way of setting out a bibliography. Your students could be asked to look in the back of non-fiction books to find some other formats.
- The bibliography used in the Student Book is fairly standard. The main point for students to remember is to be *consistent*. In other words, always put the date in the same position in a bibliography entry.

Activity 11: Credibility of sources

- Students should be realising by now that not everything printed is credible.

Activity 12: Preparing for discussion

- The discussion needs to be on something the students can resource and acknowledge. Relate the research to Social Science or another subject.

Indicator from Chapter 7: crucially examine and discuss the language of advertising; read and note down relevant persuasive features and personal responses.

Indicator: Select a claim or promise in an advertisement and write a futuristic story about the reader who has bought the advertised product or services.

Refer to *English for Melanesia Book 2*, Chapter 19.

Indicator: Read a news item of a current event and devise a relevant humorous or ironic cartoon or comic strip.

- Three sample texts are given, but any relevant current news item can be used.
- The resulting cartoons or comic strips should be displayed.

Historical development of education policy

	1960s	1970s	1980s	1990s
Process	Westernisation	Localisation	Indigenous adaptation	Indigenous development
Policy	Centralised colonial	Centralised national	Decentralised	Multilevel
Perspective	Western culture imported	Moderating Western culture	Local culture for literacy	Local culture for education
Language	English	English, restricted local language	Local language in non-formal education	Local language in formal education
Significant persons and events	G Kilalang J Gunther	Tok Pisin conference NSP research Vernacular in teachers' colleges	Philosophy of education Language and literacy section Language and literacy policy Literacy and awareness program	Education reform Literacy in-service Curriculum reform

Writing

About this strand

In the four chapters of this strand, students will practise activities that develop writing skills. When teaching writing skills, teachers need to keep in mind the language principles stated in the *Language Upper Primary Teachers Guide 2003*. For the writing strand, they are that the principles of writing are based on the belief that all students need opportunities to:

- write every day (as part of Language or another part of the curriculum),
- learn to write by writing (the teachers' role is not to talk about writing, but to provide many opportunities for students to do writing),
- learn to write by discussing their writing in pairs or groups and with the teacher,
- learn to write following models of different types of genre,
- be aware of the many different contexts and purposes of writing that are used in the real world,
- see teachers using the writing process as part of their teaching,
- have their own and other class members' writing displayed around them to create a 'print rich environment',
- have positive feedback about their progress in writing tasks,
- have time in the class to go through the whole process of writing without pressure to complete 'the product',
- have time in the classroom to share their completed writing with other students,
- be allowed to have some responsibility for the way their writing skills are developing (for example, if they can assess their own needs for paragraph development skills, they should be encouraged to refine those skills with extra tasks),
- think about the writing process,
- write for different purposes, and
- write for real audiences (for readers outside the classroom).

based on *Language Upper Primary Teachers Guide 2003*, page 6

Two key skills and processes for teaching writing are the **writing process** and using **genres**. These are outlined in the *Language Upper Primary Teachers Guide 2003*, page 11. The students have learnt about the writing process in Grades 6 and 7. Revise this process as appropriate.

Skills in using different genres are developed in all Language strands. In the writing strand, teachers should follow the four-step process in the *Language Upper Primary Teachers Guide 2003*, page 11. Activities in this four-step guide are covered in the other strands, demonstrating that writing cannot be taught in isolation.

Each chapter in the writing strand covers one of the outcomes for writing from the *Upper Primary Language Syllabus 2003*, Grade 8. The outcomes can be used to measure students' achievements in creating meaning in written language. Indicators for each outcome show the kinds of things that students should be able to do, know and understand to achieve an outcome. Indicators can be used by teachers to monitor student progress within a level and to make judgements about the achievement of an outcome. The indicators given in the *Upper Primary Language Syllabus 2003*, Grade 8, have been used as a basis for activities in the Student Book. The indicators are samples of the kind of activity you can use to check if the outcome has been reached. You should also plan other activities to use as indicators of the students' achievement of the outcome.

Many of the writing activities are integrated with speaking and listening and reading in both Language and other subjects.

The activities and materials in the Student Book are not divided into lessons. A teacher will decide on the outcome to be achieved and then select material for that outcome. Some material may be from different Language strands. The templates in the appendices will help teachers use the Student Book and this book.

Use resources in the PNG School Journals wherever possible to construct similar activities or other activities that help students achieve the learning outcomes.

Key words

These are words that you as a teacher, and your students, will be using in the four chapters of the Writing strand. You will find an explanation of the words in Appendix 7, the Glossary.

Student Book Chapter 9
risks, individual style, emotional, appeal, suitable, script, focus, immunisation

Student Book Chapter 10
connectives, conjunctions, morphemes, origin, condense, shades of meaning, review

Student Book Chapter 11
journalistic style, flashback, sequential, balanced, obituary

Student Book Chapter 12
one-sided argument, two-sided argument, neutral audience, balanced report, informative

Links to other main subjects

Student Book Chapter 9
Immunisation, Activity 7: Health

Student Book Chapter 10
Ceremonial trade, Activity 12: Social Science

Student Book Chapter 11
Social Science concepts

Student Book Chapter 12
Should species be introduced?: Social Science
Importance of preserving culture: Social Science

Possible assessment tasks

The *Language Upper Primary Teachers Guide* (pages 46–47) provides some ideas about assessing writing. The suggested areas for assessment are:

- analysis of unassisted writing samples,
- process for unassisted writing samples,
- text summaries,
- teacher-designed writing tasks,
- negotiated lists of criteria,
- journals, diaries and drafts,
- spelling checklists, and
- a general criteria sheet framework.

Teachers will assess writing across all the Language strands and other curriculum areas.

Tests for Student Book Chapter 9

Chapter 9 of the Student Book consists of examples of some kinds of writing and opportunities for students to try these kinds of writing. The examples will be kept in their writing portfolios.

For assessment in this strand, teachers will provide students with appropriate writing tasks following the examples given. When they have done the tasks, students should think about what they have learnt, and fill in the tables. Teachers can also use the tables as assessment guides.

(*Note:* This table can be adjusted so that students can grade their self-assessment as good, needs improvement etc.)

Tests for Student Book Chapter 10

Chapter 10 of the Student book considers skills and strategies for improving areas of writing. Teachers should analyse writing done by their students in terms of the outcomes.

Exercises on connectives are available in *Literacy Skills for Papua New Guinea, Improve Your Grammar Skills*, Unit 17.

Some spelling exercises are available in *Literacy Skills for Papua New Guinea, Improve Your Spelling Skills.*

I am able to react to a poem or story.	
I can see that writers put their feelings into poems and stories.	
I can record my reaction.	
I can write about my reaction.	
I can use the writing process to do this.	
I can write paragraphs that have one main point which is developed in the paragraph.	
I can summarise the plot of the story so that I can put a new event in.	
I can write notes on the characters so that the character I add fits into the story.	
I understand that sometimes there is a particular purpose for taking notes.	
I can take notes for a particular purpose.	
I can use those notes to write a paragraph.	
I can identify myths and legends by their style.	
I can write in the style of myths and legends.	
I can recognise a play by the way it is set out.	
I can correctly set out a play that I have written.	
I can recognise the way stage directions are given in a play.	
I can use stage directions correctly in my own play.	
I can turn personal notes into notes for others to read.	
I can write a variety of letters that have real purposes.	

Tests for Student Book Chapter 11

Chapter 11 considers genre and contexts.

Assessment can be done on any of the writing tasks.

Students should also self-assess either using a guide provided by you based on the outcome for the chapter, or by picking out for themselves their identified strengths and weaknesses.

Tests for Student Book Chapter 12

Chapter 12 considers language and style.

Students should self-assess. They should be able to identify the outcomes they have learnt and decide how well they have achieved the outcomes.

Teacher information

The information in this section is for you to use, if you wish, in helping you plan your lessons. You will find information on the activities and background to some activities in the four chapters of the Writing strand in the Student Book.

The *Language Upper Primary Teachers Guide 2003* (pages 28–31) provides writing strategies for the teacher to use in teaching writing. These can be applied to the activities in the Student Book. The topics covered are dictagloss, journal writing and paragraph writing (including grammar).

Students should use the writing process for all writing tasks given (see *Language Grade 6 Teacher Resource Book*) and keep all examples of writing in a writing portfolio.

You will find the answers to Student Book Activities in Appendix 6.

Student Book Chapter 9

8.3.1 Plan, and in the process take risks, to produce text with an individual style to suit a variety of challenging purposes and audiences.

Sub-strand: Production—to provide opportunities for students to use language for real purposes.

Indicator: plan with imagination and effectiveness the plot, character, and structure of own narrative writing.

Some examples of stories that take risks are given in the Student Book. Teachers should also find examples.

In order to achieve the outcome with this indicator, students need to do their own writing that takes risks with plot, character and structure in their narratives.

Indicator: plan, create and perform a short section of a story as a play-script using stage directions and setting.

This play is based on a well-known fairy tale of 'The Three Little Pigs'. Teachers could read or tell the original story first.

It should appeal to young children because

- it is humorous,
- the good characters win,
- there is plenty of action,
- the plot is not complicated, and
- there are only a few clearly differentiated characters.

These are the criteria that students should use to write their own plays.

Indicator: compare and contrast different points of view of two characters in a story.

Island of the Blue Dolphins is a Grade 7 text, but is also suitable for Grade 8. Students may find *Rice Without Rain* (Grade 8 text) a challenge.

Teachers can use other stories or novels.

The emphasis should be on the *points of view* that characters express or indicate in the stories, rather than on appearance, etc.

Indicator: write issue-based reports linked to other areas of the curriculum.

The example is given to revise the kind of information a report requires.

Revise report format with the students.

Students can use 'immunisation' to write a report, 'the dangers of smoking' as in the Teachers Guide, or another locally relevant health issue.

Indicator: create and write a play designed for young children.

This indicator has been combined with:

Indicator: plan, create and perform a short section of a story as a play-script using stage directions and setting.

The play the students write should be suitable for children. The teacher can decide the level of writing. If you have an elementary school nearby, students could present their play there, or to Grade 3 or 4 students.

Some other plays you could use as examples are *PNGSJ Senior 1*, 2001, 'The Blue Finger Disease', page 4; *PNGSJ Senior 1*, 2003, 'A Pig in The Kitchen', page 22; *PNGSJ Senior 1*, 2005, 'Naughty Billy', page 25; *PNGSJ Junior 2*, 2001, 'The Crocodile', page 18.

Indicator: devise as a class project different eye-catching posters with accurate information on the dangers of smoking for different groups of people and then contrast the different interpretations used in language and visual presentation.

Students should use the same health issue that they used for their report.

Students should be given different levels to produce their posters for; for example, for young children, for Tok Pisin or vernacular speakers, for adults with limited English, etc.

Before the posters are distributed there should be a class discussion on each poster to make sure it fits the purpose.

An example of an immunisation poster would be to make a chart with drawings of children at various ages, and the immunisations they should be getting at that age.

Student Book Chapter 10

8.3.2 Use a range of strategies and skills to respond independently and critically in order to asses their own writing and that of others.

Sub-strand: Skills and strategies—acknowledging the importance of skills and strategies necessary to effectively communicate.

Indicator: analyse meaning, spellings and use of connectives.

Other connectives that join the same kind of words or groups of words are pairs like *both/and, neither/nor, either/or*. These can join two verbs, adverbs, nouns, pronouns or adjectives.

Activity 6: Editing conjunctions

- This activity is to help students become sensitive to the fact that connective words have an important role. They help the reader come to an understanding quickly. The writer's job is to help, not hinder, the reader.
- Note that sentence 8 is more difficult as more changes are needed: At the zoo, the lions are fed the seals. → At the zoo, first the lions are fed and then the seals. *correct*
- Students may attempt to use an adverb instead of a connecting word: At the zoo, the lion are fed *before (adverb telling when they are fed)* the seals. *incorrect as a connective word, although the sentence is otherwise acceptable.*

For you to try

Allow time for feedback and discussion of the humorous or sensible sentences the students make.

Indicator: use known spellings as a basis for spelling other words with similar patterns or related meanings.

Indicator: use visual skills such as recognising common letter strings and checking critical features.

English spelling is not always easy. There is not a close relationship between speech sounds and written words. To be good spellers students need to know these important things:

- units of meaning (morphemes),
- vowels and consonants,
- common letter patterns, and
- word building patterns.

Refer to *Literacy Skills for Papua New Guinea, Improve Your Spelling Skills.*

Indicator: summarise effectively a chapter of a book in a specified number of words.

Teachers can ask for a general summary, or a summary with a purpose.

Not all answers will be the same.

To mark such summaries, do a rough outline of what you expect, and how long you expect it to be.

Indicator: write own poem experimenting with active verbs and personification and produce a poem for presentation.

Students have written many poems. Emphasise the editing process.

Indicator: plan, revise and edit writing to improve accuracy and conciseness in readiness for publication.

A book review is given, but teachers can use any kind of writing relevant to what the students are currently studying in other subjects.

Student Book Chapter 11

8.3.3 Evaluate how well own texts with different genres have been written to suit different contexts.

Sub-strand: Context and text refers to the importance of learning and using language in different situations and the fact that how we communicate influences the kind of text we use.

Activity 2: Discuss journalistic style

Indicator: *develop a journalistic style by including balance, public interest and factual considerations and compare with real life newspaper articles.*

Articles are written by professional journalists employed by the newspaper, or other people with expertise in a particular subject.

Articles are usually found inside newspapers, often near the editorial page, or in special parts of the paper, such as the *Focus* or *Weekender* pages.

Make sure students understand the difference between an article and a report. (A report should state the facts, and give opinions only as quotes.)

Newspapers have reports on news, and articles about news. Articles in newspapers are 'independent'. They are not part of the news that day, but often they make comments on the news of the day, or they discuss and give opinions about something that concerns the public.

Collect and keep a file of articles that show the characteristics of journalistic writing. These can be used to help students compare their productions with those of real life newspaper articles.

When students begin to write their own articles, emphasise the elements of:

- *Balance* (presenting both sides of an argument). Discuss whether this article is balanced—it is not really balanced as it presents only one view, that it is an admirable thing to feed starving children. A letter to the paper written a few days later criticises the article on this very point.
- *Public interest*—decide whether the public needs to know about these things; does it help in any way?
- *Factual considerations*—there is a lot of emotion in this article but the facts are there too. Any article the students write must be based on their own observation or research and have a solid basis in fact. They are, however, free to express their opinion of the facts in an article (but not a report—there, opinions can only be expressed in other peoples' words as direct quotes). They can also quote the opinion of others. Point out where this has occurred in the article ('Manna from Badili'). Refer students to a letter written in reply to this article in the Student Book appendix (passage for Chapter 2 assessment).

Activity 3: Read these biographies and Activity 4: Biographical style

Indicator: *develop the skills of biographical and autobiographical writing in-role.*

Step 1
Students should have the questions written before they begin the interview. You will need to decide the procedure and how they are going to record answers.

Step 2
Students will most likely gather more information than they need. This is a good opportunity to practice selection of material.

Step 3
Compare the structure of the biographies of Agnes and Kanage.

Some questions to help you:
Students should give their relationship to the interviewee and the circumstances in which they know them.

There should be a good reason for choosing this particular person—they admire them as a role model, their life has been interesting etc.

Estimate age if necessary by asking about important events of the time: World War II, Independence etc.

Students should find out about turning points, high points and low points.

Activity 6: A report of an accident observed

Indicator: *create two versions of a road accident witness report and then compile a police officer's overview of the incident.*

- This exercise and the obituary exercise are aimed at students learning that there can be different sides to a story. They should be able to recognise that a piece of writing can be emotive and biased, and be aware of writing bias themselves. A police report, however, should be based on facts and without bias.

Discussion:

Points of view—we all see things differently. That does not always mean that one view is right and the other is wrong. There will also be some agreement on points.

Bias—this is a stronger word and implies a sense of deliberateness.

Emotive writing—an accident is an emotional experience. Witnesses are likely to have strong feelings.

Facts—a police report needs to sort out the bias, point of view and emotion and get to the facts.

Extra exercise

Students may need some extra work on writing a report of an event. Here is an exercise based on six pictures in *Using English Students Book 1,* Grade 6, Pacific Series, OUP, pages 132–133. The pictures are in the correct order. You will need to provide a set of six pictures for students. You can use the pictures in the Grade 6 Pacific Series book, photocopy the pictures below, or draw these or another sequence of pictures on the board. The speech bubbles are not necessary for the exercise, but can be used to help students imagine what the people involved are thinking and saying.

Study these six pictures showing a road accident.

Writing

Follow these steps to write about this accident.

1. Write a report from the point of view of the cyclist.
2. Write another report from the point of view of the passenger in the car.

Now put them together to write another report the way a policeman would write it. The policeman would listen to all the witnesses. He would take notes about what each person said to him. He would try to be fair and write an accurate report without putting his own ideas or feelings in it.

Activity 9: Read two obituaries and Activity 10: Talking about obituaries

Indicator: *compose versions of an obituary written by a friend and an opponent.*

- Authentic material has not been provided in order to avoid offending living relatives.
- This exercise looks at something from two opposing points of view. There will be agreement on basic facts, but students should learn that facts can be interpreted and presented differently. Some descriptions give what is called 'faint praise', e.g. *He did his job quite well and he tried hard.*
- An alternative would be to write in-role to a friend describing someone you know well as a friend and as an opponent.
- Some adjectives can influence your thinking about a person. Teachers can give an extra exercise if they feel their students are weak in using describing words.

Extra exercise:

Sort these groups of words into positive, negative and neutral (*these are harder to find*) groups. You can use a thesaurus to increase the number of words you know. Although these words can be classed, there are degrees or gradations of positive and negative. Students could also say which words they think are stronger.

1. Appearance words: pleasant (*P*), beautiful (*P*), ordinary (*NEG*), attractive (*NEU*), ugly (*NEG*), glamorous (*P*), nice (*NEU*), good-looking (*P*), plain (*NEU*), elegant (*P*), untidy (*NEG*), dirty (*NEG*)
2. Feelings about people: like (*P, NEU*), admire (*P*), resent (*NEG*), detest (*NEG*), dislike (*NEG*), tolerate (*NEU*), know (*NEU*), despise (*NEG*), trust (*P*), esteem (*P*)
3. Facial expressions: blank (*NEU, NEG*), open (*P*), intelligent (*P*), merry (*P*), lifeless (*NEG*), lively (*P*), grim (*NEG*), sneering (*NEG*), cheerful (*P*)
4. Personality words: kind (*P*), important (*P*), popular (*P*), disliked (*NEG*), helpful (*P*), resentful (*NEG*), funny (*P*), unpleasant (*NEG*), boring (*NEG*), interesting (*P*), all right/okay (*NEU*)

Indicator: *create a story using flashback episodes of two characters involved in an event.*

Use the story 'The Small Step' in *English for Melanesia, Book 1*, page 112, to show flashback. Using flashback is a tool to make the story more exciting, and to put stress on the important parts of the story. Students could tell the story orally, in real time sequence. This will change the structure of the story considerably.

The students should now attempt to write a story with flashbacks by two of the characters. They could begin by rearranging one of the many stories in the *Senior School Journals*. These stories mostly have sequential time structures and many of them would be suitable for adaptation.

Short stories

In a short story the plot tells the reader what happens in the story and why it happens.

Sometimes an author will move the story around in time. When authors need to explain something that happened in the past that is important to the action in the story, they often use flashbacks.

For you to try

1. Write a story about an event that takes place over a period of time. This could be one hour, one day, or any period of time you like.
2. Your story should have at least two characters.

3. At some point in your story, both characters should have a flashback. That is they think back to a time that is in the past.
4. Use proper time signals so your reader will not become confused by the change in time.

Student Book Chapter 12

8.3.4 Analyse how the language and style used in their own and other writing encourages and stimulates readers to question, develop ideas and opinions, and make decisions.

Sub-strand: Critical literacy acknowledges that language learners and users need to think beyond content and recognise and evaluate the beliefs that influence texts.

Indicator: show how, in constructing effective argument, logical and sequenced points are made with good supporting evidence.

Indicator from Chapter 6: clarify the strength or the weakness of a read argument, forecast an opposing view and express this in a letter.

The arguments given in the Student Book have been adapted for the Student Book, but nonetheless, they are effective, logical and sequenced and contain good supporting evidence.

The first grass carp argument is evenly two-sided. The second grass carp argument is presented as one-sided. However, both would be based on a thorough weighing up of the evidence.

The museum argument is one-sided. You should poll the class to find who agrees. If there are disagreements, are they supportable, logical and effective?

For you to try

- Students can choose a locally or nationally important topic, or use the one developed in the Student Book.
- It is very important that they know who their audience will be.

Biological invasions

In a newspaper Focus article, the authors argued that museums have a vital role to play in the study and control of biological invasions.

The environmental and economic damage caused by the introduction of non-native species has been well studied in Australia. The cost of introduced rabbits alone is estimated to have cost the beef and sheep industries billions of dollars. The cost does not include the ecological damage the rabbits caused to the fragile environment. PNG is also susceptible to non-native invasive species. Museums should document the native fauna and flora and can provide baseline data to identify invasive species. Scientists can document the location and timing of such invasions, as well as the pattern and rate of spread of those species. This information is critical to stop or mitigate such invasions.

Indicator: demonstrate how a well-structured questionnaire with specific questions is necessary to develop good understanding of a social issue.

After reading the sample report (Activity 9), you will need to brainstorm with the class to come up with a range of suitable social issues that can be researched and reported on. Each issue you and the class agree on should be able to be researched by questionnaires, interviews, observation and library research if appropriate.

Students have learnt about questionnaires in Chapter 6.

Once they have chosen a topic to report on, they should construct a questionnaire that will help them understand a social issue.

Indicator: prepare a balanced report on a controversial issue by summarising fairly the competing views and analyse the strengths and weaknesses of them.

Refer to *English for Melanesia, Book 2*, Chapter 7.

Revise essential elements of a report.

Indicator: write a brief but informative review of a cultural activity for a local newspaper.

Collect examples from newspapers.

Revise the pyramid shape of reports. The important facts of what, who and where come first. Background and other information comes at the end.

Appendices

Appendix 1: Lesson planning table

Outcomes	**Things to work from and plan for**
1. Learning outcome	Identify the outcome in the curriculum that you are working from.
2. Content: topic or key concept	Base this on the outcomes. Decide on a theme, from other curriculum areas if appropriate, for example, our local culture.
3. What will learners learn in the particular lessons?	How will learners achieve the learning outcome? • What knowledge will they learn? • What skills will they learn? • What values and attitudes will they adopt?
4. Number of lessons that need to be taught	How many lessons do you plan to teach on this particular topic?
Assessing progress	**Things to think through**
1. Evidence of learning	What you will look for in each learner's work? Write down the assessment objectives. (Each one should be something a learner can do.)
2. The way learning will be assessed	Examples of what procedures you may use: • formal (oral or written presentation) • informal (teacher observation) • small task within a larger project • homework • test
Classroom practice	**Things to consider**
1. Method or activity	What will you do and what will learners do, and in what sequence?
2. Time	For how long will you explain or model new concepts? For how long will learners do each activity?
3. Teaching methods	How exactly will you arrange learners? • as a whole group? • working in pairs? • working individually?
4. Resources needed	Where will learners be? • in the classroom? • outside? ***List any resources you may need for students to complete tasks.***

Appendix 2: Yearly plan

Units of work	Term 1	Term 2	Term 3	Term 4
Speaking and listening	Outcome…			
	Indicator…			
Reading				
Writing				

Appendix 3: Term plan

Week	Outcomes	Student tasks	Required resources	Assessment procedures
1–3				
4–6				
7–10				

Appendix 4: Lesson plan

Teaching group √	**Required Materials**
Individual Whole class Team group	
Learning Strategies	**Specific Content—Lesson Plan Collaborating**
Interpreting Predicting Planning √ Investigating Recording √ Justifying Changing Communicating √	
Curriculum Strand	**Assessment strategy**
Cross Curricula Strands	**Cross Curricula activities**

Appendix 5: Assessment strategies

Sample 1: Cognitive skills template

LEARNING SKILLS ASSESSMENT CHECKLIST

For assessing learning skills, group communication skills and attitudes

NAME: **DATE:**

Skills	Skills observed √	Comments
Learning skills • can form and ask questions • can follow instructions • can find information • can find required information • can express ideas clearly and correctly • can critically reflect on own work • can organise oneself efficiently • understands how to improve own work • manages use of time well		
Group Skills • follows group rules • works cooperatively within a team • contributes to discussions without dominating • listens while other people speak • accommodates different points of view		
Attitudes • respects other students' points of view • participates freely in activities • works in a constructive and positive way • values the beliefs held by other students		

Sample 2: Students' own assessment of their skills development

STUDENT SELF-ASSESSMENT CHECKLIST

NAME: **DATE:**

Skills	√ Can do
My Learning Skills • I can ask questions. • I can follow instructions. • I can find the information that I need. • I can express myself clearly and correctly. • I can think about what was right and wrong about my work. • I can work neatly. • I am well organised. • I understand how to improve my work. • I use my time well.	
My Group Skills • I can work well with others in a group. • I can listen when others are talking. • I can discuss something without getting angry.	
My Attitude • I can listen and respect what others have to say. • I can take responsibility for my own work. • I can share in a group activity. • I can learn from my mistakes.	

My Comment

Appendix 6: Answers to activities in the Student Book

Student Book Chapter 1

Activity 2

5. You are amused by the unexpected answers.

Activity 4

1. To cut off an *heir* means to leave the heir without anything in a will. But *heir* also sounds like *hair*.
2. *Morning* does start at dawn, but *mourning* means that the relatives of the dead person will begin their *mourning* in the *morning*.
3. The words *told* and *tolled* sound the same; it sounds as if the pastor was speaking to or *telling* the bell.
4. The name *Humphrey* is pronounced *hump-free*, thus the camel is without a hump, or *free* of *humps*.
5. The word-play is on the similar sound of *lies* and *lice*.

Activity 5

1. Getting an A should not make you sad.
2. The chain of events is ironic.
3. Should he complain?
4. Gentle criticism.
5. The chain of events is ironic.

Activity 9

1. To summon people for feasts and ceremonial tasks, during dancing.
2. To summon people to meet the councillor, to warn people that the government officer was coming, and finally to tell that someone was dead.
3. That the traditional life is symbolically dead.
4. That it should be used only for traditional purposes; that it should be used for non-traditional purposes.
5. The old people and the young people who are receiving education.
6. The conch shell is a metaphor for the loss of tradition and changing times under mission and colonial influence.

Activity 11

1. Yes, that this is un-Melanesian, in other words, not appropriate to PNG culture.
4. The imaginative language creates a mood of sadness and reflection on where our society is going.
5. Yes, people seem to not care about each other as much as in the old Melanesian way.
6. It tells us that the passing of the old ways can be very bad for society as a whole.

Student Book Chapter 2

Activity 1

1. The first pair of sentences is disagreement; the second pair is argument (though not a good argument).
2. Disagreements do not offer reasons; arguments offer reasons.

Activity 7

positive	negative
serious	grim
youthful	immature
restful	boring
fast	hasty
fragile	flimsy
donation	handout
assertive	pushy
thrifty	miserly
inexpensive	cheap
tropical	hot

Student Book Chapter 3

Activity 2

1. One makes you think nothing went wrong, the other makes you think something went wrong.
2. Yes.
3. Yes.
4. They interpret the event from different points of view.

Activity 3

Text 1 *Title:* Donkeys are being used for taxis. The exclamation mark shows that this is thought to be surprising. *Fact:* For example, the donkey has a sign on its head. *Opinion*: Impoverished (acceptable). *The writer's opinion is not given, though the exclamation mark could be said to be opinion.*
Text 2 *Title:* Babies are not being fed properly and this is not good. *Fact:* The country's laws do protect babies from poor feeding practices, but these laws were not always followed. *Opinion*: Reporter's opinion is not given. Objective language is used. *This is acceptable for a news report.*
Text 3 *Title:* The writer thinks it is time to protest against something. *Fact:* There is a Bill which is to be put before the House next month. *Opinion*: Most of the article is opinion. *This is acceptable as the item is an editorial where opinion is permitted.*
Text 4 *Title:* Sir Michael Somare visited Goroka and the local people were happy about the visit. *Fact:* School children from Faniufa Primary School sang a song specifically composed for welcoming the guests. *Opinion*: Most of the report shows the point of view of the reporter. *The language is subjective. This is unacceptable in a news report.*
Text 5 *Title:* Someone very old is at school. *Fact:* She started taking computer classes at Richmond High in Northern California in January and is set to receive an honorary high school diploma next month. *Opinion*: The writer does not express an opinion. The language is objective. *This is acceptable for a news report.*

Activity 6

1. Against.
2. Hardworking, backbone of the country.
3. Against.
4. Dropouts take to a life of crime on the streets.
5. For example, the only strength and consolation these people have is their land.

Activity 8

Ask not what your country can do for you, but what you can do for your country.	President John Kennedy
I have a dream that my four little children will one day live in a nation where they will not be judged by the colour of their skin but by the content of their character.	Martin Luther King, Jr, 28 August 1963
We are lowering this flag, not tearing it down.	Sir John Guise, at the lowering of the Australian flag, 15 September 1975
This is one small step for man, one giant leap for mankind.	Astronauts stepping on to the moon for the first time
… we shall defend our island whatever the cost may be, we shall fight on the beaches, we shall fight on the landing grounds, we shall fight in the fields and street, we shall fight in the hills; we shall never surrender.	Sir Winston Churchill during World War II

Student Book Chapter 4

Activity 3

Powerful verbs:	General verbs:
count, break, sprouting, curves, caught, kicking, stabs, merges	walk, gone

Activity 4

a) The dog rushed to *fetch* get the ball from the sea.

b) The tourist *sauntered* walked through the craft market and inspected the items that had been *displayed* put there.

c) After the snake *slithered* came in the door it *slid* went under the table. (Or the other way round.)

d) My wantok *coaxed* got me to lend him K50, then *vanished* went.

e) 'I'm sorry, the plane was scheduled to *depart* go at 6 a.m.,' *apologised* said the announcer.

f) As we *strolled* walked along the beach on our science trip, we *observed* saw many crabs *scurry* go into holes in the sand.

g) 'I broke the chair,' *admitted* said Ravu.

h) The angry man *stalked* walked into his office and *hurled* put his bag on the desk.

i) 'Hey, your bike *splashed* put some mud on my dress,' Sabua *complained* said.

j) At first water *seeped* went onto the road slowly, then the pipe *burst* and it *gushed* went quickly.

Activity 7

3. Non-verbs are: tattered, rippling, broken, seeping, carved, frightening. They are functioning as adjectives.

Activity 8

past tense	present tense	future tense
travelled, paddled	are …tied, are paddling, paddle, decides, paddle, says, moves, mutter, are hurting, complains, drift, are, snaps, duck, seize, go, stabbing, yells, do (not) fight, keep moving, is, am seeping, can feel, (is) gathering, (is) trickling, want, look, is enjoying, chews, goes, is, think, reach, looks, save, (we are to …), let, go, changes, turns, look	won't be, will stay, should be

1. Present.
2. To make the story feel immediate, so that the listener is involved in the story.

Activity 9

1. am/is/are + verb + -ing
2. Now, in the present, as the sentence is being spoken.

Activity 10

The sentences are all in the present continuous tense form, but they are not all performing a present function.

a) He *is meeting* her tomorrow. *future*
b) She *is always running* away. *A repeated habit—it is not happening right now.*
c) They *are travelling* to Manus next week. *future*
d) 'Where are you, Mum?' 'I *am* in the kitchen, *cooking* taro for dinner.' *present*
e) Just think about what it was like. It is late at night. I *am standing* at the window … *Referring to a story from the past*
f) Now I *am adding* the water to the flour. *present (instructions in a demonstration)*
g) He *is chopping* the wood. *present*

Activity 13

2. Regally, approvingly, vividly.
3. They are adverbs of manner. They add information by telling in what manner an action was done: *strode regally; nodding approvingly; can vividly recall.*

Activity 14

1. Tau *grinned* at the teacher.
2. Sera and Rawali *ambled* to the beach.
3. The headmaster *glared* at the chicken.
4. We *raced* towards the finishing line.
5. Koki and Geno *whispered* at the back of the meeting.

Activity 15

a) The books were put down everywhere.
b) We borrowed the books yesterday.
c) We sometimes swim in the rough sea.
d) We worried about our grandmother during the storm.
e) Sibona lay next *to* the tree.
f) I never walk under mango trees when the wind is blowing.

Activity 12

present		past	
present simple	**present continuous**	**past simple**	**past continuous**
are	are determining	was	were tasting
has	are showing	submitted	were judging
has	is tasting	said	were entered
is	is detecting	spurred	
make		did	
remains		won	
		said	

Activity 17

Commas separate items in a list. Note that sometimes there will be a comma before the 'and' and the last word in a list.	List all the present simple, past simple, present continuous and past continuous verbs.
Commas act like brackets around a phrase or word that needs to be separated from the rest of the sentence, or around additional information in a sentence.	'On those days I make six runs,' said Avni Mullai, fifty years old, a former farm worker.
Commas separate parts of a sentence (clauses) and show a small pause for the speaker.	List the words that look like verbs, but are not functioning as verbs.
Commas are used after introductory words in a sentence.	For example, the legislation says that a prescription from a doctor is necessary to buy things for bottle-feeding.
Commas are used in direct speech. They separate the spoken words from the unspoken words.	'The plane was scheduled to go at 6 a.m.,' apologised the announcer.
Commas come after words such as 'Hey,'.	'Hey, your bike put some mud on my dress,' Sabua said.
Commas separate a name when it is the name of the person being spoken to. 'Tupa, I want you to … .'	'Peta, yu go long dua.'
Commas separate the two parts of a tag question.	You know what work commas do in sentences, don't you?

Student Book Chapter 5

Activity 1 questions

1. This is amusing.
2. Through the character of Chase.
3. Someone who can 'read' the thoughts of others and predict what will happen.
4. She always seems to know what he is doing and thinking.
5. Because we know that his mother is just normal and is basing her words on what she knows usually happens.

Activity 2 questions

1. Happiness that the girl seemed to have accepted herself.
2. Sadness that the girl did not feel part of her family.
3. Yes, as the misunderstandings are cleared up.
4. Through the language she uses: *outsider* is a very strong word.
5. Through the language she uses: *longed for, loved.*

Activity 3 questions

1. Anger and sadness.
2. A dying fire.
3. Fire, embers, Hollywood, coconut frond.
4. That culture is dying, the 'fire' has gone out, only embers remain—can it be revived, or is it overwhelmed by introduced fashion?
5. Yes—the images are strong and the symbols give another meaning to the poem.

Activity 4

Questions for Poem 1

1. s
2. Alliteration.
3. It adds to enjoyment of the poem.
4. Because people associate it with snakes.

Questions for Poem 2

1. For example: scattering, scurrying; blustering, bullying, bellowing.
2. For example: gusty and dusty.
3. Student's choice.

4. Enjoy the feeling of movement it gives.
5. Yes.

Activity 5

Questions for Poem 3

1. Full rhyme: leaf/reef; boy/joy.
2. Near rhyme: arm/worm; isle/soil.
3. No: Verse 1 abab; Verse 2 aabb.
4. They make the reader feel the rhythm of the poet's thoughts.

Questions for Poem 4

1. Less.
2. Lines 2 & 4; 6 & 8.
3. Yes.
4. They make the reader feel the rhythm of the poet's thoughts.

General questions

1. Rhyme pattern for 'A Song of the Wind' is aabccbddbaab; many of the rhymes are -ing words.
2. Rhyming poems are easier to respond to because of the patterns they have; often the response is pleasurable.

Activity 7

1. a) he was anxious to learn.
2. a) her parents did not care for her well.
3. b) they were waiting for a ship to come.
4. c) the people were hard working and interested in the welfare of their village.

Activity 9

1. Heat, fire, sun glazed, shimmer, scorched.
2. Because it was specifically mentioned.
3. That it is not mechanised.
4. That the harvest is poor (the grain stalks do not have many grains on them; the people are not happy).

Activity 10

The older the violin, the sweeter the music it makes.	Some things become more beautiful with age.
A thin person is not necessarily a hungry person.	A person can have more than is first obvious.
The canoe has gone over the waterfall; it can't come back up again.	Some things that you do can't be undone.
The stone lying on the cool river bed never dreams that it's hot above.	Poor people often can't believe that rich people have problems too.

Activity 11

1. People of the same kind like to stick together.
2. A person who is not willing to take responsibility for his mistakes.
3. Don't assume that you will be successful before it is certain.
4. Not all things suit the same people. Some may like something, while others hate it.
5. You must live with the consequences of your actions.

Activity 12

2. The story can be seen as outlining different points of view, as a fable, or as a moral for the world. Your local actions can affect the world: 'Think globally, act locally.'

Student Book Chapter 6

Activity 1

a) 1945.

b) To spread the news about the struggle for independence.

c) Java.

d) Wayang kulit.

e) Patriotic leaders, independence fighters, civil servants, governors, Dutch colonists, Japanese soldiers and common people.

f) In the 1920s.

g) To help spread Islam and tell about the history of the sultans.

Activity 4

Question type	Question number (1–6) from the questionnaire
Categorical questions—these ask you to make a choice of two options, based on your opinion	6
Fill-in questions—these ask for facts about you.	1
Open-ended questions—these ask you to write your own response.	5
Scaled response questions—these ask you to record how strongly you feel about something	4
Ranking questions—these ask you to put your choice in order	2
Checklist questions—these ask you to tick one or more of a number of choices offered.	3

Activity 5

1. Unclear questions: To what extent would you use the library? (What does 'extent' mean in this context?)
2. Questions which ask the person filling in the questionnaire (*respondent*) to remember things: How many books did you read last year?
3. Questions which ask for an answer the person filling in the questionnaire may not know: How many books are there in the school library?
4. Double questions: Do you like newspapers and books?
5. Questions which lead the person filling in the questionnaire towards an answer: Do you think libraries are useful?
6. Questions using language that is hard to understand: Do you ever use the Dewey Decimal system to locate a book?

Activity 11

fuzzy-minded idealist	a person not in contact with real life
quack	a pretend doctor
bleeding heart	a person who is always feeling sorry for wrongdoers
egghead	an intelligent person
cowboy	a rough sort of person

Activity 13

Cartoon 1

1. Malaysian.
2. Yes.
3. The way to get around threats is to bribe people.
4. The land owners are shown as small; they want development.
5. The Forest Minister is shown as big; he is telling the Malaysian to keep 'eating' trees; stereotype of greed, ready to be bribed.
6. An indication of relative importance and power.

Cartoon 2

1. An MP.
2. Fat stomach, drinking, smoking, taking his ease, not listening to the small people.
3. An indication of relative importance and power.
4. Greedy, lazy, not concerned about little people.
5. There is some truth and stereotypes have their uses, but can also be abused.

Student Book Chapter 7

Activity 2

1. No flashbacks, a straight chronological timeline.
2. No gaps, the reader is with the characters all the time.
3. He goes into town proudly with his family.
4. He realises that having a new car is not so wonderful after all, and that, old though the truck is, it has its uses.

Activity 4

1. Early to mid-morning.
2. Yes.
3. No flashbacks.
4. Yes: we are left to infer that Craig takes his bike to the bathroom and works on it there until afternoon. *After lunch* … there is a gap in the action.
5. She sees that Don values her brother and does not want Don to think that she doesn't get on well with her brother; she is putting on good behaviour in front of her boyfriend; maybe she thinks she will go too when Craig goes to fix the car.

Activity 6

1. Shortly before Independence Day.
2. One year later, shortly before Independence Day.
3. No.
4. One year.
5. Yes, some paragraphs refer to an earlier time period.
6. Yes, between the end of the discussion with neighbours and the race day; between the end of the race and shortly before the next Independence Day.
7. No, probably not.
8. Yes, because she treats it sympathetically.

Activity 8

1. During the morning or afternoon.
2. Only a short time after it starts.
3. Yes, apart from the flashback.
4. Probably about one hour.
5. Yes, to the death of Huria.
6. No, we are with the characters in real time.
7. From the point of view of the old man; the author has adopted this persona to tell the story.
8. Yes, the inference is that he will die soon.

Activity 11

1. 1: explanatory; 2: instructional; 3: persuasive.
2. 1: Weather Office Explains King Tides; 2: How to Make a Leaf Boat; 3: We Can Feed the World—Here's How.
3. 1 explains how something works; 2 gives step-by-step instructions with diagrams; 3 gives a point of view and supports it with persuasive language.
4. Yes.

Student Book Chapter 8

Activity 2

1. The main point is found at the end of the passage: that learning a language and learning to read and write are not the same.
2. Children learn complex aspects of language before age 5.
3. You do not need to be literate to discuss complex ideas.

Activity 4

1. Literacy rates: total M/F, rural/urban M/F, by province M/F.
2. The rate varies between males and females. In all cases the female rate is lower than the male rate. The rates for rural and urban areas are different. The rates for provinces are different. The rates improved from 1990 to 2000.
3. Yes, because women often pass on learning to children.
4. Students' own questions.
5. Tables, line graphs, pie graphs.

Activity 6

Graph 1

1. Tells about people who have attended school, separate male and female information.
2. *Vertical:* percentage of citizen population. *Horizontal:* ages in groups of five years, beginning with 5–9 and ending with 75 plus.
3. 5–9.
4. 10–14.
5. Male.
6. They will be lower.

Graph 2

1. Shows the difference in attendance at school between rural and urban sectors.
2. *Vertical:* percentage of citizen population. *Horizontal:* ages in groups of five years, beginning with 5–9 and ending with 75 plus.
3. 10 years.
4. Urban.
5. Urban rates will be higher.

Activity 8

1. Reading.
2. No.
3. Because they are learnt in the same way.
4. Meaning and communication.
5. 'That's my <u>friend</u>. My friend is <u>clever</u>. I <u>like</u> my <u>friend</u>.'
6. Yes.
7. No.
8. Constant use of functional language.
9. To help children who are not familiar with print. They see it as a less threatening situation because they don't have to learn a new language (English) at the same time.
10. Familiar situations.

Activity 10

1. Six.
2. Because the author of this book was quoting from them, and using information and ideas that belong to others.
3. Alphabetical order.
4. Surname or second name first, first name second, date of publication third.
5. The name of the writer is not given.
6. Because government publications do not usually give an author.
7. Newspapers.
8. The name of the publisher, where it is published, that it is the Australian edition.

Activity 11

1. He is employed by a research institute and is a senior person there.
2. It is based on collected data and put together by experts.
3. Textbooks can sometimes be biased, it is best to find out more about the authors if possible.
4. No, sometimes the reporter gives a bias to the report.
5. Yes.
6. No.

Activity 13

1. K40 free!!!
2. It makes you read on.
3. A loan scheme.
4. Best; you only; feel the difference; customised; competitive; efficient; fast; hassle free; same day service (also Hurry!—this word gives you the idea that you need to do this now to get the best benefit).
5. The use of exclamation marks.

Activity 14

1. Two.
2. In speech bubbles above their heads.
3. Two.
4. They are like paragraphs.
5. To trim the sails means to set them to catch the wind, not to cut pieces off with scissors.

Student Book Chapter 9

Activity 2

Telephone Call by Joy Cowley

1. Mrs Webb's.
2. By Mrs Webb's responses.
3. A neighbour? a rat catcher? a council man? a plumber?
4. He was scared of the rat.
5. A fun story; the rat is obviously not real.

The Man Who Never Fin … by Graham Jackson

1. Finished (anything).
2. Unfinished, uncomfortable in their surroundings, vague.
3. Boat, letter box.
4. Bill Smith.
5. The story is written in present tense. Stories are usually written in past tense.
6. It is unfinished.

The Blue Humber 80 by Jack Gabolinscy

1. Left home.
2. Yes.
3. No.
4. No, because they have to save very hard to buy the car.
5. No.
6. Because he felt he had let down and disappointed his son.

Activity 3

Telephone Call by Joy Cowley

1. No, not in dialogue form like this.
2. No.
3. No.

The Man Who Never Fin … by Graham Jackson

1. No.
2. No.
3. You feel sorry for him?

The Blue Humber 80 by Jack Gabolinscy

1. No.
2. No.
3. No.
4. By realistic description.

Student Book Chapter 10

Activity 1

1. and
2. or
3. but
4. so

Activity 2

1. Connective *words* can join words, for example, aibika or aupa; or *groups of words*, for example, stared at the bone and snarled at us.

2. *and* joins two verbs (verb phrases).
3. *or* joins two nouns.
4. *but* joins two adjectives.
5. *yet* joins two adverbs.
6. *or*.

Activity 3

1. before
2. because
3. when
4. wherever

Activity 4

1. before tells the order.
2. because tells the reason.
3. when tells the time.
4. wherever tells the place.
5. put at the beginning of sentences. They still do the work of connective words.

Activity 6

1. The sun shone brightly *after* the mist cleared.
2. The goal-keeper was clumsy ~~and~~ *but* speedy.
3. The game will go ahead, *unless* the weather gets worse.
4. As children we liked fishing *and* also hunting butterflies.
5. Do you want kaukau ~~and~~ *or* would you prefer rice?
6. *Because* we felt sorry for the cat, we fed it. (Or *so we fed it.*)
7. ~~When~~ *Unless* it rains, we have soccer practice every day.
8. At the zoo, the lions are fed *before/after* the seals.

Activity 7

1. The 'g' is not sounded in sign, but is sounded in signal and signature.
2. Photo/graph, pho/tographer, photo/graphic—different parts of the words are stressed, and the letters are broken in different places.
3. The 'c' in medicine has a soft sound, the 'c' in medical has a hard sound and the 'c' in medicinal has a soft sound.
4. The 'o' is a sound short in cloth and a long sound in clothes and clothing.

Activity 8

1. judge, judgement, judicial, judicious
2. connect, connection, connective
3. migrate, migrant, emigrant, immigrate, immigration, migration, migratory
4. horrid, horrible, horrific, horrify, horror
5. navy, naval, nautical, navigate
6. write, writer, writing
7. event, eventful, eventual, eventually
8. magnify, magnificent, magnitude

Activity 10

school: from the Greek *schola* (learned discussion)
fortnight: running together the words *fourteen nights*
thirteen: from the Anglo-Saxon *threteen* (three and ten)
calendar: from the Roman word *calendarium* (account book)
scone: from the Dutch word *schoon-brot* (fine bread)

Activity 11

1. alligator
2. alphabet
3. family
4. graffiti
5. tattoo
6. umbrella

Activity 12

Possible answer:
The purpose of Kula Ring gift exchanges in Milne Bay is to encourage trade and friendship.

In the western highland areas, however, Moka, Mok-ink and Te exchanges are more about establishing status within the clan and with other clans.

Activity 14

1. spread, soar, seek, spy, fear
2. yes
3. yes

Activity 15

1. sing, laugh, cut, whistle

Activity 16

(There may be other opinions)

1. smile, chuckle, giggle, laugh, hoot
2. crawl, stroll, walk, trot, march, gallop
3. surprise, intrigue, amaze, appal, horrify
4. whisper, talk, shout, shriek, roar
5. hum, croon, sing, yodel, bray
6. glimpse, glance, look, stare, gaze

Student Book Chapter 11

Activity 2

1. Newspaper readers who want more than just a report of facts, who want to explore ideas a little.
2. In this case it is to highlight a problem and the kindness of the women. Often the journalist wants to bring something to the public attention. Also he or she writes to help to sell the newspaper, thus the writing can be emotional and exaggerated, and use words designed to make the reader feel in a certain way (in this case, sorry for the children).
3. Yes, it has many elements which would suit the public interest: pathos, relief that the reader is not one of the children, desire to help. (The story provoked a lot of reaction in the form of letters to the editor and further comments.)
4. The headline makes the reader want to read the article. The journalist gives vivid

Activity 17

The story of *Island of the Blue Dolphins* is set in the past on an island off the coast of California. The island environment … *comment on the setting (time and place) if it is important*
The theme of *Island of the Blue Dolphins* is survival. We see that it is possible for a person to live alone for many years and yet remain human. The main character, Won-a-pa-lei … *show that you understand the theme of the novel*
The main character of Won-a-pa-lei makes many decisions that are important turning points in the story. For example, she decides to leave the island because she was afraid of the wild dogs. *give examples from the story to show that you can support your comments*
The author builds up the suspense towards the meeting of the two girls by … *show that you can see something of the way the author achieves the effects in the story*
It is not until after Ramo is killed by wild dogs that Won-a-pa-lei … *show that you understand the sequence of events in the story*
As a character, Won-a-pa-lei grows and changes without outside influences. Despite the setbacks she suffers she continues to survive. When her canoe is destroyed, for example, she gathers wood for another one. On page … she "…" *describe character and how it develops in the story, giving examples and quotes*
I felt that I would not have survived as well as Won-a-pa-lei did. *talk about your personal reaction to the events, theme or characters in the story.*
We are given a picture of the effects of traditional beliefs on Won-a-pa-lei. For example, she believed that the winds would take away her breath if she made weapons, or that the weapons would break in her hands. *comment on important aspects of the story which give you information about the life of the characters*

descriptions and uses 'our story' to involve the reader.

5. It should catch your interest and make you want to read the report or article and convey some indication of the content. Often the headline is sensational or contains a language joke.
6. Manna is what falls from heaven in the Bible to feed the hungry. Here the 'manna' falls from some women in Badili. There is also a mention of angels.
7. Pity for the children, admiration for the women who feed them.
8. The children come from all over PNG. Tauri Robert comes from Goilala. He is about six years old.
9. There are many opinions, for example, 'This may seem like a small event on a national scale, but to the children, the people who feed them are "angels".'

Activity 6

Question 5

a) My friend and I were standing on the corner, at the intersection of Kulau and Mango Roads.

b) First we saw a man on a bicycle coming towards us.

c) He was followed by a car and a truck.

d) On our right there was a man in a car driving very fast and he was not looking where he was going.

e) The bicycle, car and truck were on his right, so he should have given way to them, but he was stupid and didn't stop.

f) When he saw the bicycle, he put on his brakes and skidded.

g) The car went into the path of the car and truck on Mango Road.

h) The car behind the bicycle slammed on his brakes and skidded sideways.

i) The truck behind the car couldn't stop in time and hit the two cars.

j) The man on the bicycle was not hit, and he just rode away down Mango Road.

Appendix 7: Glossary

Student Book Chapter 1

gentle irony humorous comment using irony, not to be confused with sarcasm

subtle humour humour that arouses quiet amusement, not slapstick or humour that provokes gales of laughter

pun a play on words

spontaneous without preparation

improvise do something without preparation

message the essential information needed for understanding to take action

creative imaginative or out of the ordinary, in order to arouse interest and attract attention

sensitive being aware of the feelings of others, empathy and sympathy; acting and speaking in a manner appropriate to the situation

cultural reference mentioning a particular culture to enhance speech or writing

extended metaphor a metaphor that is used for a few sentences, a paragraph, a short story or even a whole novel

Student Book Chapter 2

discuss talk and listen in a group and exchange ideas

agreement a state of agreeing with a suggestion

disagreement a state of not being able to agree on a topic

effective argument an argument that clarifies and persuades

problem the basic issue in a conflict

clarify work towards making something as clear as possible

respect in an argument, to listen to the other person without putting them down

perceptions ways of looking at things, points of view, awareness of other people's feelings

empathy putting yourself in another person's place and trying to see things from their point of view

conflict situation where there are opposing views

reduce make smaller, make less of a problem, make less significant

acknowledge give an indication that you are aware

win–win a situation in which both sides of a conflict are happy with the result

negotiate give and take, talk through a problem to find an acceptable solution

confronting aggressive

connotation the additional meaning a word gets through general usage

so-called a confronting way of referring to an idea

opponent the person who you are arguing against

conciliation coming together peacefully

compromise a halfway point between two opposing points of view

synthesis mixing things together to make something different

Student Book Chapter 3

manipulate deliberately try to alter or change

effect (noun) /affect(verb) to use something for effect is to use it in a way that will make the listener or reader react

effective how successful something is in having an effect

impartial not showing bias, not on one side or the other

impartiality the state of being impartial

objective factual language, feelings not involved

subjective emotional language, showing feelings

challenging making you think about your own ideas, controversial

language context the kind of context in which the language is being used, such as personal or political

Student Book Chapter 4

satire	exaggeration to make fun of something. Satire can also be used to hurt.
powerful	arouses feelings or gives a strong image
form	the structure of the verb tense. For example, regular verbs are formed by adding -ed for the past simple tense.
function	the work of the word in the sentence. For example, a word that looks like a verb could be functioning as an adjective.
tense	how a verb shows when something happens
manner	how something is done, as indicated by using an adverb

Student Book Chapter 5

respond	react with some feeling
response	the way you react with some feeling
influence	a degree of control over something
symbol	something that stands for something else
theme	the message behind the words and images
sound	the linking of sounds in a poem—poetry is meant to be read aloud. Sound can form a pattern in a poem.
alliteration	the linking of words that begin with the same sound
assonance	the linking of vowel sounds within words
rhyme	linking sounds at the end of lines (and also within lines: interior rhyme)
full rhyme	words that sound the same except for a single sound at the start of the word
near rhyme	words that sound almost like a rhyme
rhyme pattern	poets use the same sounds at the end of words to create a pattern which is often regular
infer	to think of meaning beyond the words that are written or heard
folk saying	a saying that comes from a culture, like an idiom
proverb	an idiomatic sentence
metaphor	a comparison of two things to form an image
alternative	another way
memorable	staying in your memory
enduring	lasting a long time

Student Book Chapter 6

questionnaire	a series of questions designed to give certain information
response	the answer given and recorded
respondent	the name for a person who fills in a questionnaire or gives answers in an interview
categorical	question where the respondent must choose one option or the other—there is no grey area or scaling
scaled	instead of a categorical yes or no, the respondent is allowed to wholly or partly agree or disagree
ranking	putting answers in order from most acceptable to least acceptable, or least to most acceptable

Student Book Chapter 7

flashback	an incident in a story that happens before the main narrative time line
time period	the length of time in which action happens
real time	as if it were happening at that time
persona	the 'person' who speaks, thinks and acts in the story—they need not be anything like the author
genres	different types of writing that have their own specific features
implications	events that can happen as a result of an action
consequences	events that can happen as a result of an action
green revolution	a surge in agricultural production

Student Book Chapter 8

functional language language which does not have meaning on its own, but functions to form sentences—the words have functions, for example, *my* functions as a first person possessive pronoun

fluent speaking or writing freely, easily and correctly

source a text you use in your own work. This can be any sort of text: written, visual, oral or from an interview

citing the act of telling what the text used is

quote to take words from a text (oral or written) without changing them

paraphrase to put a text into your own words—of course it must still be acknowledged

credible believable, well-known, expert

plagiarism unacknowledged use of ideas or facts

acknowledge to make reference to the text source

bibliography a list of texts used in a discussion, essay, report etc.

format the way of setting something out on the page

futuristic imagination abut the future

Student Book Chapter 9

risks to go outside the safe zone that you are accustomed to

individual style a style that is your own, evolved over a period of experimentation

emotional to do with your feelings

appeal reaching out to a need or feeling

suitable matching the need

script the dialogue and stage directions needed for a play

focus turn attention to a particular thing

immunisation protect by vaccination against certain diseases

Student Book Chapter 10

connectives words that connect other words or groups of words

conjunctions connecting words such as *and*

morphemes units of meaning in words

origin where something first came from

condense make shorter

shades of meaning subtle differences

review write an analysis of something read

Student Book Chapter 11

journalistic style comment on an issue or news for the reader who wants more than straight facts, which could include opinion and/or exaggeration

flashback return to a past event

sequential time frame when events are written about in the same time order as they occur in reality

balanced not biased

obituary a tribute to the life of a person who has recently died

Student Book Chapter 12

one-sided argument showing one viewpoint only

two-sided argument showing awareness of the opposite viewpoint to that held by the writer

neutral audience an audience that does not have strong or fixed opinions about an issue

balanced report a report that considers both sides of an issue fairly

informative providing useful, relevant, appropriate and accurate information

Acknowledgments

The author and publisher wish to thank the following copyright holders for granting permission to reproduce their material.

The National newspaper, for 'UNICEF paints grim picture of health services', *The National*, 24/08/05 and 'Charities work on wheelchairs' (adapted), *The National*, 23/09/05.

The author and publisher would also like to acknowledge the following sources:

Theresa George for her poem 'Golden Arms', published in *Using English, Grade 6, Book 1, The Pacific Series*, Oxford University Press, 1980, p 67;

Every effort has been made to trace the original source of copyright material contained in this book. The publisher would be pleased to hear from copyright holders to rectify any errors or omissions.